Inhalt

W0471754

Unit 6

Unit 7

Revision C (Unit 6–7)

Unit 1

Zahlen

1 Schreibe die folgenden Zahlen auf Englisch aus.

1	______________	30	______________
6	______________	36	______________
9	______________	44	______________
12	______________	55	______________
18	______________	80	______________
21	______________	83	______________
28	______________	100	______________

Sich kennenlernen

2 Was fehlt hier? Setze die passenden Wörter in den Dialog ein.

Hello. ______________ name is Ann. — Hello.

What's ______________ name? — John.

How ______________ are you? — I'm twelve.

______________ are you from? — I'm from Paris.

______________ your phone number? — It's 863 2119.

Personenbezeichnungen

3 Ordne die durcheinandergeratenen Buchstaben zu Personenbezeichnungen.

yob ______________________ takecarer ______________________

cheater ______________________ rotut ______________________

umm ______________________ eifndr ______________________

gril ______________________ luipp ______________________

Verben

4 Finde die zehn englischen Verben in dem Wortgitter und schreibe sie neben die entsprechende Übersetzung.

r	l	i	s	t	e	n
e	p	l	a	y	p	f
a	r	h	w	o	k	i
d	r	a	t	e	p	n
w	r	i	t	e	h	d
q	a	c	a	g	o	b
s	h	o	u	t	n	v
a	u	p	y	f	e	m
y	i	y	m	a	k	e

abschreiben *to* ______________________ zuhören ______________________

finden ______________________ machen ______________________

sagen ______________________ schreien ______________________

schreiben ______________________ anrufen ______________________

lesen ______________________ spielen ______________________

In der Schultasche

5 Sieh dir das Bild an und schreibe auf, welche Gegenstände du siehst.

______________________ ______________________

______________________ ______________________

______________________ ______________________

____

Das englische Alphabet 1

6 Höre genau hin und schreibe die Wörter auf, die buchstabiert werden.
Tipp: Alle Wörter haben mit der Schule zu tun!

1. ______________________ 7. ______________________
2. ______________________ 8. ______________________
3. ______________________ 9. ______________________
4. ______________________ 10. ______________________
5. ______________________ 11. ______________________
6. ______________________ 12. ______________________

Das Klassenzimmer

7 Beschrifte die neun Gegenstände, die du auf dem Bild siehst.

Präpositionen

8 Schau dir das Bild von Übung 7 nochmals an und vervollständige dann die Sätze.

The apple is __ the table.

The pencils are ______ the table.

There are some books __ the cupboard.

There is a poster __ the wall.

The chair is _______ the desk.

Classroom phrases

9 Vervollständige die folgenden Redewendungen für den Unterricht.

S_r_y _‘m _a_e.

S_t _o_n, _l_a_e.

Y_u‘_e _e_c_m_.

W_a_‘s _o_ h_m_w_r_, p_e_s_?

C_n _ g_ t_ t_e _o_l_t, p_e_s_?

W_e_e _r_ w_?

Eigenschaftswörter

10 Übersetze die Eigenschaftswörter und schreibe sie waagrecht in die Kästchen. Die Buchstaben in den grauen Feldern ergeben das Lösungswort.

höflich
anders
langweilig
beängstigend
richtig
groß
glücklich
leicht

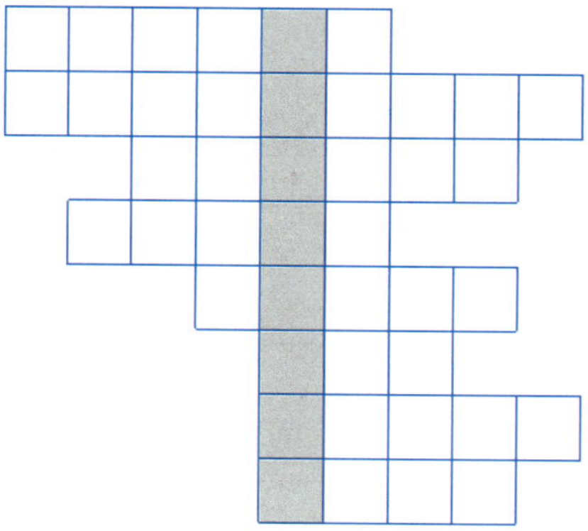

→ English is not ______________________________.

Die Personalpronomen und die Langformen von *to be*

To be heißt „sein". Hier findest du alle Formen auf einen Blick.

Singular:	**I am** Terry.	**Ich bin** Terry.
	You are twelve.	**Du bist** zwölf.
	He is nice.	**Er ist** nett.
	She is my friend.	**Sie ist** meine Freundin.
	It is a mouse.	**Es ist** eine Maus.
Plural:	**We are** in year six.	**Wir sind** in der 6. Klasse.
	You are cool.	**Ihr seid** cool.
	They are OK.	**Sie sind** in Ordnung.

11 Finde die sechs Personalpronomen, die sich in dem Kasten verstecken, und übersetze sie.

I	s	i	t
t	h	e	y
w	e	p	o
o	h	e	u

______________ ______________

______________ ______________

______________ ______________

Tipp

You hat drei Bedeutungen: „du", „ihr" oder das Anrede-„Sie"! *Are you happy?* kann also bedeuten „Bist du glücklich?", „Seid ihr glücklich?" oder „Sind Sie glücklich?"

12 Trage die fehlenden Formen von *to be* ein.

I ________________ eleven.

This is Emma. She ________________ my friend.

We ________________ from London.

Hello John. You ________________ in my tutor group.

John ________________ from Bristol.

My new school ________________ big.

That is Francisco and this is Maria. They ________________ from Spain.

13 Bilde Aussagesätze, indem du die Wörter in die richtige Reihenfolge bringst.

are – they – nice ________________________________

is – she – here – new ________________________________

my – is – friend – Tom ________________________________

am – eleven – I ________________________________

Lisa – is – this ________________________________

14 Übersetze die folgenden Sätze ins Englische.

1. Sie ist meine Lehrerin. ________________________________
2. Henry und William sind nett. ________________________________
3. Ich bin in deiner Klasse. ________________________________
4. Fußball ist mein Lieblingssport. ________________________________

Die Kurzformen von *to be*

Es gibt auch Kurzformen von *to be*. Sie werden hauptsächlich bei Personalpronomen und in der gesprochenen Sprache verwendet.

Singular	**Plural**
I'**m** eleven.	We'**re** here.
You'**re** nice.	You'**re** my friends.
He'**s** my tutor.	
She'**s** new.	They'**re** from London.
It'**s** old.	

15 Schreibe die Sätze neu, indem du die Kurzform von *to be* verwendest.

1. They are in the classroom. ______________________
2. It is a football. ______________________
3. I am from Madrid. ______________________
4. You are in the wrong room. ______________________
5. We are eleven. ______________________

Kurz- oder Langform? 2

16 Höre dir die Sätze an und vervollständige die Lücken. Achtung: Hörst du die Lang- oder die Kurzform?

______________ in Year 5.

______________ nice.

______________ in my tutor group, too.

______________ in my bag.

______________ late.

Die Verneinung von *to be*

Auch bei der Verneinung von *to be* gibt es sowohl Lang- als auch Kurzformen:

Langformen	**Kurzformen**
I am not eleven.	**I'm not** eleven.
You are not nice.	**You aren't** nice.
He is not my friend.	**He isn't** my friend.
She is not here.	**She isn't** here.
It is not a mouse.	**It isn't** a mouse.
We are not in the classroom.	**We aren't** in the classroom.
You are not new here, girls.	**You aren't** new here, girls.
They are not in my tutor group.	**They aren't** in my tutor group.

17 Verneine die folgenden Aussagen in der Langform.

1. I am eleven. ______________________
2. It is a football. ______________________
3. They are late. ______________________
4. You are my friend. ______________________
5. She is from Greenwich. ______________________

18 Schreibe die richtigen Wörter in der Kurzform in die Lücken.

Maria ____________ ten. ____________ eleven.

Rob ____________ from London. He ____________ from Cardiff.

They ____________ pupils. ____________ teachers.

That's a book. It ____________ a poster.

Fragen und Kurzantworten mit *to be*

Wenn du eine Frage mit einer Form von *to be* bilden möchtest, stellst du einfach Subjekt und Verb um – genau wie im Deutschen.

Frage	bejahte Kurzantwort	verneinte Kurzantwort
Am I in your class?	Yes, you are.	No, you aren't.
Are you from London?	Yes, I am.	No, I'm not.
Is he nice?	Yes, he is.	No, he isn't.
Are they eleven?	Yes, they are.	No, they aren't.

19 Bilde aus den angegebenen Wörtern Fragen.

are – late – we – ? ______________________________

friend – he – is – your – ? ______________________________

shoes – they – are – your – ? ______________________________

20 Verbinde die Fragen jeweils durch eine Linie mit der passenden Antwort.

Am I lucky?	Yes, they are.
Is he from Greenwich?	No, I'm not.
Are they new here, too?	Yes, you are.
Are you always late?	No, he isn't.

21 Ergänze die fehlenden Formen von *to be* in der Frage und die passende Kurzantwort dazu.

__________ you a teacher? – No, ____________________.

__________ that your pen? – Yes, ____________________.

__________ they in your bag? – No, ____________________.

Der unbestimmte Artikel

Im Englischen gibt es zwei Formen des unbestimmten Artikels: *a* und *an*.

That's **a b**ag.	That's **an o**ld shoe.
Is this **a p**encil?	Is that **an e**xercise book?

Beginnt das folgende Wort mit einem Konsonanten, steht der unbestimmte Artikel *a*. Vor einem Vokal verwendet man *an*, außer wenn das *u* als [ju] ausgesprochen wird: Bei *unit* ['ju:nɪt] etwa steht ***a*** *unit*.

22 *A* oder *an?* Trage den passenden unbestimmten Artikel ein.

Is that _________ English book? – No, it's _________ German book.

Here's _________ sandwich and here's _________ apple.

That isn't ________ pen. It's ________ old pencil. It's _______ useful thing.

Der bestimmte Artikel

Die Aussprache des bestimmten Artikels *the* – *der/die/das* ändert sich je nachdem, was für ein Buchstabe vorausgeht:

the [ðə]	**the** [ði:]
the **b**ook, the **t**utor group,	the **E**nglish girl, the **a**pple,
the **u**nit [ju:nɪt]	the **e**xample

→ Vor Vokalen wird *the* mit einem langen „i" ausgesprochen.

Die Aussprache von *the* 3

23 Höre genau hin und kreuze an: Hörst du *the* als [ðə] oder als [ði:]?

	[ðə]	[ði:]		[ðə]	[ði:]		[ðə]	[ði:]
1.	☐	☐	4.	☐	☐	7.	☐	☐
2.	☐	☐	5.	☐	☐	8.	☐	☐
3.	☐	☐	6.	☐	☐			

Die Pluralformen der Nomen

Du bildest die Pluralform der meisten Substantive, indem du einfach ein ***s*** an die Singularform hängst: *one book – two book**s**.*

Nach **stimmlosen** Lauten wie *f, p, t, k,* θ wird die Endung [s] ausgesprochen: *two groups, three units, six marks*

Nach **Vokalen** und **stimmhaften** Lauten wie *b, d, g, l, m, n, v* lautet sie [z]: *four balls, five bags, holidays*

Achtung: Nach Zischlauten wie *-s, -ss, -sh, -ch, -x* lautet die Pluralendung ***-es***: *sandwiches, buses, bushes.* Sie wird [ɪz] ausgesprochen.

Aussprache der Pluralendungen 4–5

24 Höre dir an, welche Pluralformen gesprochen werden, und ordne die Wörter dann der richtigen Aussprache der Endung zu.

[s]	[z]	[ɪz]
____________	____________	____________
____________	____________	____________
____________	____________	____________

25 Ordne die Wörter der richtigen Aussprache zu und überprüfe dann mithilfe der CD, ob deine Antwort richtig war.

books **desks** **exercises** **numbers** **pages** **friends** **games** **lists** **sandwiches**

[s]	[z]	[ɪz]
____________	____________	____________
____________	____________	____________
____________	____________	____________

There is …/There are …

Achte darauf, *there is* und *there are* nicht einfach mit „da ist/da sind" zu übersetzen. Im Deutschen gibt es eine Reihe verschiedener Wiedergabemöglichkeiten:

There is a book in the cupboard.	Im Schrank **befindet sich** ein Buch.
There's a girl on the chair.	Ein Mädchen **sitzt** auf dem Stuhl.
There are three posters in my room.	In meinem Zimmer **gibt es** drei Poster.
There are two pencils on the desk.	**Es liegen** zwei Bleistifte auf dem Schreibtisch.

26 Ergänze *there is* oder *there are.*

____________ twenty classrooms in the school. ____________ twelve tables in one classroom. ____________ a bag on one table. ____________ a book in the bag. ____________ fifty-five pages in the book. On one page ____________ a picture. In the picture ____________ a school.

27 Sieh dir das Bild an. Was liegt alles auf dem Tisch?

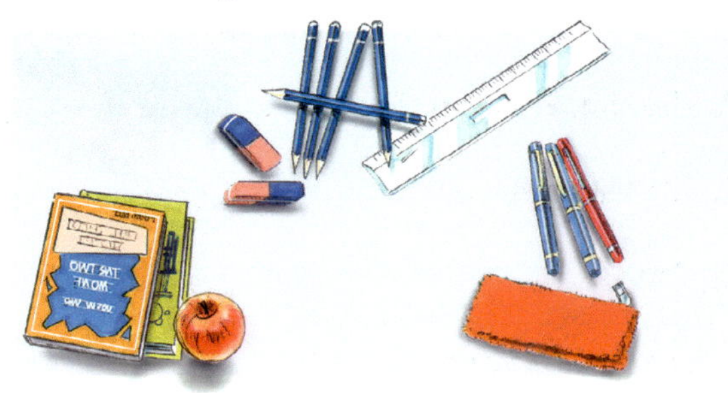

There are two exercise books.

____

____

Die Fragewörter *where, who, what* und *how*

Präge dir die folgenden Fragewörter ein:

Where are you?	I'm in the classroom.	→ *Wo?*
Where is he **from?**	He's from London.	→ *Woher?*
Who's he?	He's Peter.	→ *Wer?*
What is that?	It's my exercise book.	→ *Was?*
How old are you?	I'm eleven.	→ *Wie?*

28 Füge die passenden Fragewörter ein.

_______________ is that? – It's a mouse.

_______________ are you ____________? – I'm from Greenwich.

_______________ is that? – It's Lisa.

_______________ old are you? – I'm eleven.

_______________ is the teacher? – She's in the classroom.

_______________ is on the desk? – There are two books.

29 Übersetze die folgenden Fragen ins Englische.

1. Wo ist dein Apfel? ______________________
2. Was befindet sich auf dem Tisch? ______________________
3. Wer ist im Klassenzimmer? ______________________
4. Wie alt ist Tom? ______________________
5. Woher kommt der Lehrer? ______________________
6. Wer ist Mr Cash? ______________________

Informationen heraussuchen

30 Gemma schreibt einer Freundin in Bath eine E-Mail und erzählt ihr darin von der Schule und ihren neuen Freunden. Lies den Text durch und kreuze an, ob die Aussage richtig oder falsch ist.

Hi

My new school is big and scary but my tutor is nice. Her name's Mrs Seddon and she's my English teacher, too. The classroom is big but there are nice posters on the walls. My new friends are very nice. David is in my tutor group and he's good at football. Sally isn't in my tutor group but she's in Year 7, too, and her jokes are cool. Sally isn't good at football and her football is now in the caretaker's room.

	richtig	falsch
1. Gemmas neue Schule macht ihr Angst.		
2. Gemmas Klassenlehrerin unterrichtet auch Deutsch.		
3. An der Wand des Klassenzimmers hängen große Poster.		
4. David und Sally sind beide in Gemmas Klasse.		
5. Sally ist nicht gut in Fußball.		
6. Sallys Fußball ist jetzt im Zimmer der Hausmeisterin.		

31 Schreibe die richtigen Ziffern neben die englischen Zahlen, rechne das Ergebnis aus und schreibe es wiederum als englische Zahl aus.

five	______	fifteen	______	forty-four	______
+ seven	______	+ ten	______	+ thirty-three	______
+ eight	______	+ thirteen	______	+ two	______
= ______	______	= ______	______	= ______	______

Das Wesentliche verstehen

32 Sieh dir das Bild von Gemmas Klassenzimmer genau an, dann lies die drei Beschreibungen durch und wähle die richtige aus.

A) My classroom is big and there are three big windows. There's a table under one window and there's a mouse under the table. There are pens and pencils on the table. There's a cupboard under a window and there are some books in the cupboard. There's a football in the cupboard, too. There are eight nice posters on the wall and there are eleven desks in the classroom. There are chairs behind the desks.

B) My classroom is big and there are three big windows. There's a table under one window and there's a mouse on the table. There are rubbers and a ruler on the table, too. There's a cupboard under the window and there are some books in the cupboard. There's a football in the cupboard, too. There are seven nice posters on the wall and there are eleven desks in the classroom. There are chairs behind the desks.

C) My classroom is big and there are three big windows. There's a table under one window and there's a mouse on the table. There are pens and pencils on the table, too. There's a cupboard under the board and there are some books in the cupboard. There's a football in the cupboard, too. There are eight nice posters on the wall and there are eleven desks in the classroom. There are chairs behind the desks.

→ Beschreibung ____________ stimmt mit dem Bild überein.

Hören und schreiben 6–7

33 Höre dir den Dialog auf der CD an und trage die fehlenden Wörter in die Lücken ein.

Nicola: Look. There's Paul.

Fiona: Is he ________________ here?

Nicola: Yes, he is. He's from Manchester. He's ________________.

David: Cool? No, he isn't. His jokes are ____________________.

Nicola. No, they aren't. And he's nice.

Fiona: Is he in Year 7, ________________?

Nicola: Yes, he is, but he ________________ in my tutor group.

Fiona: And what's his ______________________________ sport?

Nicola: It's football. And this is his __________________.

David: Oh, good. Let's ________________ now.

Nicola: But David. Paul isn't your ____________________.

David: Oh. ________________ OK.

34 Höre dir die folgenden Sätze an und schreibe die Zahlen auf, die du hörst.

Hi. I'm Jackie and I'm ________________. Ann is my friend and she's ________________. I'm at Greenwich School and it's very big. There are __________________ classrooms in my school. There are _________________________ pupils in my class and we're lucky – there are ________________________ chairs. Mr Ellis is my teacher. He's ________ ____________________.

Hören und überprüfen 8

35 Lies zuerst den Dialog und bringe dann die Sätze in die richtige Reihenfolge, indem du sie nummerierst. Danach höre dir den Dialog auf der CD an und prüfe, ob du richtig liegst.

Yes, he is. He's cool.	☐
Yes, I am. I'm in Mr Carter's tutor group.	☐
Hi. I'm Emma. What's your name?	☐
My name's Jimmy. Are you in Year 7, too?	☐
I'm from Madrid. Is Mr Carter nice?	☐
Oh, good. Mr Carter's my tutor, too. Where are you from?	☐

Hören und verstehen 9

36 Lies zunächst die folgenden Aussagen durch. Dann höre dir den Dialog auf der CD an. Welche der Aussagen sind richtig, welche falsch?

	richtig	falsch
1. Phil is from Cardiff.		
2. Cardiff isn't nice.		
3. Kylie is in Phil's tutor group.		
4. Kylie's bag is on the chair.		
5. All Phil's friends are in Cardiff.		

Unit 2

Die Familie

1 Sieh dir den Stammbaum der Spencers an und setze dann die richtigen Wörter in die Lücken.

Look at Tracy Spencer's family ____________. She has got a big family. Sarah Spencer is her ____________. Tim Spencer and Rachel Smith are her ____________. They have got three ____________. Tracy's ____________ is David Spencer and he is ____________ from her ____________, Elena Stavros. She has got one ____________, Samuel, and he is an ____________ child. Tracy isn't an only child. She has got one ____________, Phil and one ____________, Susan.

Zu Hause

2 Beschrifte die Bilder.

1. u ____________

d ____________

w ____________

d ____________

g ____________

2.

s ____________

3.

f ____________

s ____________

3 Bilde Wörter aus den Buchstaben, um herauszufinden, was sich alles in Stevens Zimmer befindet.

e – d – b ____________

a – o – s – f ____________

d – m – r – u – s ____________

a – b – e – t – l ____________

r – a – o – w – r – d – b – e ____________

e – c – r – m – u – p – o – t ____________

e – e – t – l – i – i – v – o – n – s ____________

Länder und Nationalitäten

4 Finde die sieben Länder, die sich in dem Wortgitter verstecken.

R	W	E	N	G	L	A	N	D
U	G	G	R	E	E	C	E	G
S	A	T	U	R	K	E	Y	R
S	Y	K	C	M	J	H	Z	E
I	P	F	R	A	N	C	E	E
A	L	B	T	N	E	L	D	K
I	T	A	L	Y	I	A	X	N

5 Ergänze die Adjektive zu den Ländernamen.

England

Germany

Greece

Italy

France

Russia

Turkey

Verben und Ausdrücke

6 Finde die passenden Verben zu den Sätzen und trage sie in das Wortgitter ein.

1. Let's … to a CD.
2. … the words and numbers.
3. … your books, please.
4. … the sentences with the names.
5. Annie can … Lisa.
6. … your name.
7. Let's … a game.

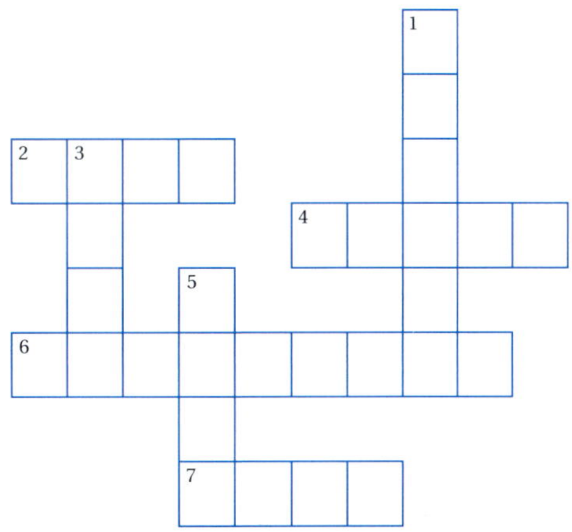

7 Bilde vollständige Sätze, indem du die Satzteile mit einer Linie verbindest.

I'm interested	good with dogs.
My brother	in music.
She's in a	up.
What	is a pain.
How can I	a mess.
Let's take	turns.
Let's have	hurry.
My sister is	a party.
She is fed	do my homework?

Adjektive und Substantive

8 Schreibe die Adjektive, die sich in der Buchstabenschlange verbergen, neben ihre Übersetzung.

klein ________________ großartig ________________

schön ________________ glücklich ________________

langsam ________________ albern ________________

beschäftigt ________________ leise ________________

schmutzig ________________

9 Im Klassenzimmer. Baue aus den Wortteilen ganze Wörter zusammen und schreibe sie in die richtige Lücke.

gro	maga	pro	mus	pho	id
zine	ea	to	up	ject	ic

Let's look at a ____________________.

Let's read a ____________________.

I've got an ____________________.

Let's play in a ____________________.

I can finish my ____________________.

Let's listen to ____________________.

Der *s*-Genitiv

Singular

Pat**'s** cat is old. — Pats Katze ist alt.
Mr Watt**'s** flat is small. — Herrn Watts Wohnung ist klein.
The dog**'s** ball is red. — Der Ball des Hundes ist rot.

Steht das Substantiv im Singular, folgt beim Genitiv **Apostroph + *s*.**

Plural

The boy**s'** bags are big. — Die Taschen der Jungen sind groß.
The girl**s'** dad is nice. — Der Vater der Mädchen ist nett.
The Hiltons' house is new. — Das Haus der Familie Hilton ist neu.

Steht das Substantiv im Plural und hat bereits ein Plural-*s*, fügst du an dieses *s* nur noch den **Apostroph** an.

10 *'s* oder *s'*? Ergänze die richtige Endung.

Helen ___ book is great.

The Elliot ___ flat is over a shop.

The pupil ___ names are John and Jill.

Tom ___ drums are in his bedroom.

The girl ___ T-shirts are in her wardrobe.

11 Übersetze diese Sätze.

1. Die Hausaufgabe der Jungen ist leicht.

___

2. Der Name der Katze ist Tiger.

___

3. Helens CDs sind auf dem Tisch.

___

4. Die Fotos des Mädchens sind in ihrer Tasche.

___

Die Possessivbegleiter

Possessivbegleiter zeigen an, wem eine Sache gehört:

Singular

my – mein	I'm Jenny and this is **my** brother, Chris.
your – dein	You are late and where's **your** bag?
his – sein	He's my friend. **His** name is Robert.
her – ihr	She is good at sport. This is **her** football.
its – sein	It's my school. **Its** classrooms are big.

Plural

our – unser	We're sisters. **Our** parents are in the house.
your – euer	You're nice, girls, and **your** brother is nice, too.
their – ihr	John and Henry are my brothers and there are **their** bikes.

12 Schreibe die richtigen Possessivbegleiter in die Lücken.

I'm Susan and this is _______ sister. _______ name is Ann.

Is that _______ dog, Ben? – Yes, it is, and that's _______ ball.

Phil and Chris, what's _______ dad's name? – _______ name is Theo.

There are my cousins. They're in _______ garden.

Possessivbegleiter oder Personalpronomen? 10

13 Höre dir die Sätze an und füge die Possessivbegleiter oder die Kurzform von *to be* mit dem Personalpronomen ein.

____________ silly and ____________ jokes are funny.

____________ my friends and ____________ house is next to my house.

That's our house. ____________ small but ____________ garden is big.

____________ new here and ____________ sister is in my tutor group.

Have got/has got

Langformen	**Kurzformen**
I **have got** one brother.	I**'ve got** one brother.
You **have got** a big house.	You**'ve got** a big house.
He **has got** a new CD.	He**'s got** a new CD.
She **has got** a nice T-shirt.	She**'s got** a nice T-shirt.
It **has got** big windows.	It**'s got** big windows.
We **have got** a dog.	We**'ve got** a dog.
You **have got** a new teacher.	You**'ve got** a new teacher.
They **have got** four cousins.	They**'ve got** four cousins.

14 Schreibe die richtigen Langformen von *have got/has got* in die Lücken.

My name is Kevin. I ________________ one sister and one brother. We ________________ a house in Greenwich. It is small but it ________________ a big garden. My sister ________________ her own room but my brother and I are in one room. That's a problem. My parents ________________ a computer shop and so we ________________ five computers in our house. I ________________ three mice, my sister ________________ a cat and my brother ________________ a dog. They are not friends.

Lang- oder Kurzform? 11

15 Höre dir die Sätze auf der CD an und schreibe auf, was du hörst.

________________ a green house. ________________ a new CD.

________________ a nice stepfather. ________________ a big problem.

________________ three televisions.

Die Verneinung von *have got/has got*

Langformen	**Kurzformen**
I **have not got** a sister.	I **haven't got** a sister.
You **have not got** a new CD.	You **haven't got** a new CD.
He **has not got** a bike.	He **hasn't got** a bike.
She **has not got** a grandad.	She **hasn't got** a grandad.
It **has not got** a garden.	It **hasn't got** a garden.
We/you/they **have not got** a car.	We/you/they **haven't got** a car.

16 Schau dir die Bilder an und schreibe *'ve got/'s got/haven't got* oder *hasn't got* in die Lücken.

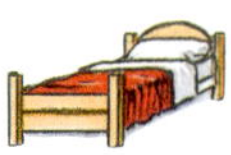 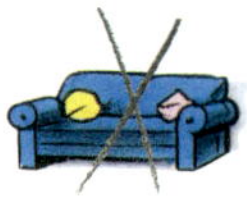

I ________________ a bed but I ________________ a sofa in my room.

She ________________ a table but she ________________ a computer in her room.

They ________________ a bike but they ________________ a football in their shed.

He ________________ a wardrobe but he ________________ drums in his room.

Kurz- oder Langform? 12

17 Höre genau hin: *'ve got/'s got/haven't got* oder *hasn't got?*

I ________________ a pen but I ________________ a pencil.

She ________________ new shoes but she ________________ a new T-shirt.

Fragen und Kurzantworten mit *have got/has got*

Have you got a brother?	**Yes, I have.**
Has Jane got a new T-shirt?	**No, she hasn't.**
Has Tom got a big room?	**Yes, he has.**
Has the cat got a mouse?	**No, it hasn't.**
Have we got a new teacher?	**Yes, we have.**
Have the girls got a grandad?	**No, they haven't.**

18 Baue aus diesen Wörtern in der richtigen Reihenfolge Fragen oder Sätze.

a – TV – you – your – got – have – in – room – ?

____

not – has – Susan – two – sisters – got

____

got – your – house – big – has – windows – ?

____

two – have – CDs – I – got – new

____

19 Formuliere Kurzantworten.

Have you got two grandads?	Yes, ________________
Have your cousins got a big house?	No, ________________
Has Lizzie got new shoes?	Yes, ________________
Has your garden got a shed in it?	No, ________________

Der Imperativ

Mit dem Imperativ forderst du jemanden auf, etwas zu tun:
Open the window, please.
Be quiet, Tony.
Write your names here, please.
Für ein Verbot oder eine Warnung brauchst du das Hilfsverb *don't:*
Don't talk now, girls.
Don't play your drums, please.
Don't read the answers, boys.

20 Kate und Glenda haben für ihre Eltern eine Liste mit Regeln erstellt. Formuliere Sätze mit dem Imperativ.

open the wardrobe	✗	do our homework	✓
watch out in here	✓	read our exercise books	✗
use our computer	✗		

____

____

____

____

____

21 Übersetze diese Befehle.

1. Wechselt euch ab. ______________________
2. Bitte seien Sie leise. ______________________
3. Spielt hier nicht Fußball. ______________________

Das modale Hilfsverb *can*

Can bedeutet „können" oder „dürfen". Die Kurzform der verneinten Form *cannot* (Achtung Zusammenschreibung!) ist *can't*.

Aussagen

I **can** play the drums.
Linda **can** listen to my CD.
They **can** play football here.

You **can't** use my chemistry set.
He **cannot** do the homework.
We **can't** open the door.

Fragen

Can I look at your photos? – Yes, you can.
Can you read Spanish? – No, I can't.
Can Annie use your pen? – Yes, she can.

22 Schau dir die Bilder an. Was können oder dürfen die abgebildeten Personen machen und was können oder dürfen sie nicht machen?

play football ✗
play the drums ✓

She ______________________ but she ______________________.

write on the board ✓
write on the wall ✗

They ______________________ but they ______________________ ______________________.

talk ✗
listen ✓

The cat ______________________ but it ______________________.

23 Schreibe Kurzantworten zu den Fragen.

Can I use your mobile, please? – No, ______________________.

Can Emma write a sentence in Turkish? – Yes, ______________________.

Can we have a party? – No, ______________________.

24 Übersetze diese Fragen und Kurzantworten und verwende dabei die Langformen von *can*.

Darf ich deine neue CD anhören? – Ja, klar.

___

Dürfen wir im Gartenhäuschen spielen? – Nein, das dürfen wir nicht.

___

Kannst du mein Handy in deine Tasche legen? – Ja, kann ich.

___

Kann dein Opa einen Computer benutzen? – Ja, das kann er.

___

Können Sie einen Satz auf Französisch sagen? – Nein, aber ich kann einen Satz auf Russisch sagen.

___

___

Can oder *can't*? 13

25 Höre dir die CD an und schreibe *can* oder *can't* in die Lücken.

I ______________ do my homework.

You ______________ draw in my book.

She ______________ listen to music in her room.

Tom ______________ play this game.

We ______________ have a party.

Jackie ______________ help you.

Informationen heraussuchen

26 Elliot schreibt über seine Familie. Lies erst den Text, dann die Sätze und entscheide, ob sie richtig oder falsch sind.

I have got a big family. I have got two sisters and a half-brother. My dad is divorced from my mum and my mum is now married to Juan. My half-brother's name is Pablo and he's Spanish. His dad is Spanish, too. I can now say three sentences in Spanish. Pablo's OK but we are in one room and that's a problem. My sisters are in one room, too, because we've got a small house. We've got a garden, too. There's a shed in the garden but we can't play in the shed because it's very small.

1. There are five people in Elliot's family. ____________
2. Juan is Elliot's step-father. ____________
3. Elliot can't say words in Spanish. ____________
4. Elliot is in one room with Pablo and his sisters. ____________
5. They've got a small house with a garden. ____________
6. They can play in the shed. ____________

27 Wie sind diese Personen mit Melanie verwandt?

Bill is Melanie's ____________.

Christine is Melanie's ____________.

John is Melanie's ____________.

Das Wesentliche verstehen

28 Diane hat einen Aufsatz geschrieben. Lies zuerst den Text durch, dann weise den Absätzen die richtige Überschrift zu.

My room   Rules   My house   My family

____

I've got one sister and one brother. My brother's name is Nicholas and he's eight and my sister's name is Joanne and she's twelve. I am eleven. My sister's great. I can read her magazines and listen to her CDs. My brother is nice, too. His jokes are funny.

____

Joanne and I are in one room but that isn't a problem. We can talk and play in our room. My brother has got his own room but it's very small. We've got a garden and there are two big trees in it. Nicholas has got his own small house in one tree.

____

My room is big and there are two beds, a wardrobe, a table and a computer in it. There are some posters on the wall and there's a big window. We haven't got a TV in our room but there's a TV downstairs.

____

My parents can't come in our room and they can't use our computer. Nicholas can't play football in our room and he can't look in our wardrobe, but he can come in and play. Joanne can't take my CDs but she can listen to the CDs in our room. We can all play games together. It's nice.

29 Lies den Text nochmals und beantworte die Fragen mit „ja" oder „nein".

1. Mag Diane ihre Familie? ________________
2. Kann Diane in ihrem Zimmer Fernsehen schauen? ________________
3. Darf Nicholas in ihr Zimmer gehen? ________________

Hören und nachsprechen 14

30 Mark redet mit einer Lehrerin über sein Zuhause. Höre zu und sprich die Sätze nach.

Hören und schreiben 15

31 Lies die Kurzdialoge durch und überlege, was in die Lücken passt. Höre dann die CD an und ergänze die richtigen Wörter.

– Mike, ___________ I ___________ in your room, please?

– Yes, you ___________, but ___________ use my computer.

– I'm not ___________. I ___________ find my bag.

– Oh, I can ___________ you.

– Thanks. Let's ___________ in my room.

– Oh no. What a ___________!

– Ann, have you ___________ my new T-shirt?

– No, I haven't, but ___________ got my discman.

– No, I ___________. ___________ got it.

– Dad?

– Hey! ___________ play with my drums.

– Oh, please. ___________ I play with ___________?

– Oh OK.

Hören und das Wesentliche verstehen 16

32 Höre dir die Dialoge an und schau die Bilder an. Welches Bild passt zu welchem Dialog?

1.

Dialog ____________

2.

Dialog ____________

3.

Dialog ____________

4.

Dialog ____________

Hören und Informationen heraussuchen 17

33 Janet besucht Tina zum ersten Mal. Höre dir den Dialog an und schreibe „richtig“ oder „falsch“ neben die Sätze.

Tinas Zimmer ist groß. ____________

Tina findet, dass ihr Bruder nervt. ____________

James’ Zimmer ist sehr ordentlich. ____________

Tina und Janet spielen Computerspiele in James’ Zimmer. ____________

Dann machen sie in James’ Zimmer ein Fest. ____________

Janet findet, dass James nicht nett ist. ____________

Unit 3

Hobbys

1 Suche die acht Wörter aus dem Wortgitter, die mit Freizeit zu tun haben.

c	o	o	k	i	n	g	n	b
l	a	f	w	t	u	i	p	i
u	c	i	n	e	m	a	q	k
b	d	l	s	a	j	s	w	e
u	b	m	s	e	h	x	b	m
m	s	w	i	m	m	i	n	g
l	u	e	n	j	w	p	t	z
p	e	y	g	u	i	t	a	r
d	a	n	c	e	a	v	c	g

______________ ______________

______________ ______________

______________ ______________

______________ ______________

2 Was kannst du in deiner Freizeit tun? Verbinde die Verben mit den richtigen Substantiven.

watch	a game
play	a book
read	a song
go	a film
ride	a bike
sing	to the cinema
play	swimming
go	the guitar

Tipp Wenn möglich, lerne zum Substantiv gleich das passende Verb. Dann hast du immer die passende Wendung parat!

Alltag

3 Ein ganz normaler Tag. Sortiere die Sätze der Reihe nach passend zu den Uhrzeiten.

I eat my lunch. **I go home.** **I go to bed.** **I go to school.** **I go to sleep.** **I have breakfast.** **I get up.** **I wash my face.** **I wake up.**

7.30	______________	12.30	______________
7.35	______________	15.30	______________
7.40	______________	20.30	______________
7.45	______________	20.45	______________
8.15	______________		

4 Freitag: Henry beschreibt seinen Tagesablauf. Ergänze die passenden Verben.

go to bed **walk** **walk the dog** **feed** **eat** **visit** **watch**

On Fridays I get up and then I ______________ my dog. He always has breakfast first! Then I ______________ to school. I usually ______________ sandwiches at school for lunch. After school I always ______________ first and then I sometimes ______________ friends. In the evening I often ______________ TV and then I ______________ late because we have no school in the morning.

Wann? Wie oft?

5 Wie viel Uhr ist es? Vervollständige die Sätze.

at half past three **at the weekend** **pm** **from ... to**

when **on Tuesdays** **What time is it, please?**

____________________________ – It's half past nine.

What time is the computer club? – It's __________ three thirty

__________ half past four.

What day is cooking club? – It's ____________________.

__________ can we meet? – How about ____________________?

We start school at 9 o'clock and we always go home __________________.

I often fall asleep at 9 __________.

6 Wie oft? Schreibe die Wörter in der richtigen Reihenfolge auf.

always__________________ 100

____

____

____

____________________ 0

sometimes **often** **usually** **never**

Wichtige Verben

7 Fülle die Buchstabenlücken auf.

sich erinnern — to r _ _ e _ _ e _

vergessen — to f _ _ g _ _

mögen — to l _ _ e

lieben — to l _ _ e

schauen — to l _ _ k

8 Finde die Verben im Wortgitter und trage sie in die richtigen Sätze ein.

w	u	c	a	l	l
g	t	h	f	s	o
t	e	a	c	h	o
s	x	s	t	o	k
a	k	e	o	w	i
b	r	i	n	g	c
p	m	z	r	n	k

Can you ____________________ me your photos?

We often ____________________ a football in the park.

I can ____________________ you a trick.

Can you ____________________ me my bag, please?

Dogs often ____________________ cats.

You ____________________ nice.

My cat always comes when I ____________________ her name.

Nützliche Redewendungen

9 Bilde Sätze aus den angegebenen Teilen und setze sie in die passenden Dialoge ein.

See you	It's Emma	How are	He's	There	It's time
she is.	here.	there.	to go home.	great fun.	you?

OK. We can meet at 10 in the park. – Great. ______________________

______________________ – I'm OK, thanks.

Hi. ______________________ – Oh, hi. Where are you?

Can we watch a film now? – No. ______________________

Can you help me? I can't find Molly. – Yes. Oh, look! ______________________

Is Paul nice? – Yes. ______________________

10 Übersetze die nützlichen Redewendungen in blau.

That was a good trick. He can't believe his eyes.

____

What about lunch? Can you eat at school?

____

I can't meet you on Friday but how about Saturday?

____

What's on TV?

____

Die Uhrzeit

Es gibt zwei Methoden, die Uhrzeit auszudrücken:

9.00	It's nine o'clock.	It's nine o'clock.
9.05	It's five past nine.	It's nine-oh-five.
9.08	It's eight minutes past nine.	It's nine-oh-eight.
9.10	It's ten past nine.	It's nine ten.
9.15	It's quarter past nine.	It's nine fifteen.
9.20	It's twenty past nine.	It's nine twenty.
9.30	It's half past nine.	It's nine thirty.
9.35	It's twenty-five to ten.	It's nine thirty-five.
9.45	It's quarter to ten.	It's nine forty-five.
9.50	It's ten to ten.	It's nine fifty.
9.56	It's four minutes to ten.	It's nine fifty-six.

It's 2 am. – Es ist zwei Uhr morgens.
It's 2 pm. – Es ist zwei Uhr nachmittags.

11 *What time is it, please?* Formuliere die Uhrzeit auf beide Arten.

1.15	__________	__________
6.40	__________	__________
3.12	__________	__________
9.35	__________	__________
2.25	__________	__________
8.30	__________	__________
11.55	__________	__________
10.48	__________	__________

12 Formuliere die Uhrzeit um.

1. We start school at **nine fifteen.** quarter past nine
2. It's **ten forty-eight.** ______
3. The bus goes at **three thirty.** ______
4. He gets up at **seven forty-five.** ______
5. We go swimming at **five twenty-five.** ______
6. We can meet at **one forty.** ______
7. She wakes up at **six fifty-five.** ______
8. I feed my dog at **four-oh-five.** ______

Tipp Vergiss nicht: 8.30 ist *half past eight* im Englischen, aber „halb neun" auf deutsch!

Wie spät ist es? 18

13 Höre dir auf der CD an, welche Uhrzeit genannt wird, und zeichne sie auf der Uhr ein.

1. 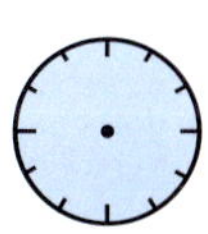	2. 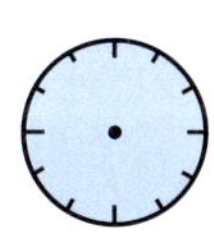	3. 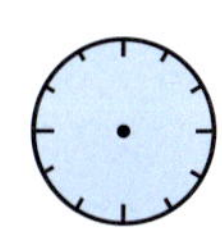
4. 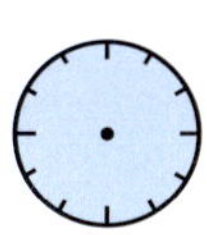	5. 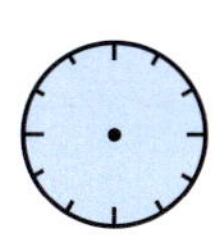	6. 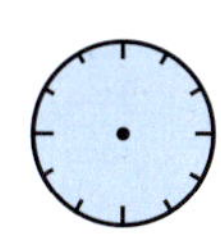
7. 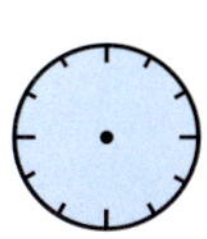	8. 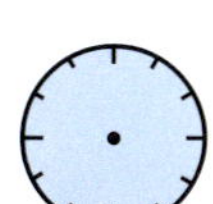	9. 

Die einfache Form der Gegenwart

Bei *I*, *you*, *we* und *they* hat die einfache Form der Gegenwart dieselbe Form wie der Infinitiv:
I watch TV in the evening.
You sometimes watch a video.
We never watch TV in the morning.
You watch a film at the cinema.
They watch a video at the weekend.

14 Übersetze die folgenden Sätze.

1. Ich stehe um 8 Uhr auf.

___

2. Am Dienstag gehst du nie schwimmen.

___

3. Wir gehen immer zu Fuß zur Schule.

___

4. Ihr spielt am Wochenende Schlagzeug.

___

5. Sie spielen Fußball im Park.

___

6. Patrick und Sophie hören Musik.

___

Das *-s* in der 3. Person Singular

Bei der 3. Person Singular, also *he, she* und *it*, hängst du ein ***s*** oder ***es*** an das Verb an. Aussprache:

[s]	Jill sometimes sleep**s** late.
	She often meet**s** her friends.
[z]	John feed**s** his dog in the morning.
	Then he run**s** to school.
[ɪz]	Ella wash**es** her face every morning.
	School finish**es** at 3.30.
[gəʊz]	Martin often go**es** to the park on Saturday.
[dʌz]	Janet always do**es** her homework in the evening.

15 Kylies Tag. Lies dir die Verben durch und entscheide dann, welches Verb wohin gehört. Achte auf die richtige Endung!

to go **to do** **to feed** **to get up** **to go home** **to finish**

to start **to meet** **to play** **to wash** **to watch**

Kylie ______________ at 7.30 and then ______________ her face. She has breakfast and then ______________ her cat. She ______________ to school at 8 o'clock because school ______________ at 8.30. School ______________ at 3.15 and Kylie ______________ again. Sometimes she ______________ her homework then and sometimes she ______________ her friends in the park. In the evening she often ______________ games with her brother and sometimes she ______________ TV.

16 Gebe Kylies Aussagen in der dritten Person wieder.

I like dancing.

I never teach my brother tricks.

I often go to the cinema.

She ____

____

____

Die Aussprache des End-s 19

17 Schau dir zunächst die Verben an. Wie würdest du sie aussprechen? Trage sie in die Spalten ein und überprüfe dann deine Antworten mit der CD.

to call – to chase – to forget – to finish – to get up – to happen – to like – to love – to remember – to run – to sleep – to teach – to walk – to wash – to watch

[s]	[z]	[ɪz]
______________	______________	______________
______________	______________	______________
______________	______________	______________
______________	______________	______________
______________	______________	______________

Tipp Vergiss nie: *He, she, it* – das *s* muss mit!

18 Meine Schwester und ich. Ergänze die Verben in blau mit der richtigen Endung.

My sister and I are very different. She ______________ (to like) cats and I ______________ (to like) dogs. She ______________ (to get up) early and I ______________ (to get up) late. She ______________ (to walk) to school but I ______________ (to run). She ______________ (to do) her homework at home on her desk. I ______________ (to do) my homework at school in the playground. She always ______________ (to wash) her face but I often ______________ (to forget). She ______________ (to go) to dancing lessons and I ______________ (to play) football. But, yes, I am a girl, too.

Die Satzstellung in Aussagesätzen

Die grundsätzliche Satzstellung im englischen Aussagesatz ist
Subjekt – Verb – Objekt: Kevin rides a bike.
Aussagesätze mit einer Zeit- oder Ortsangabe:

	Subjekt	Verb	Objekt	
In the evening	I	watch	TV.	
	I	watch	TV	**in the evening.**

Aussagesätze mit einem Häufigkeitsadverb:

Ann	**never**	gets up	early.
We	**often**	play	tennis in the park.
Grandad	**sometimes**	writes	on my computer.

Aussagesätze mit Hilfsverb und Häufigkeitsadverb:

I am	**never**	late for school.
We can	**sometimes**	ride our bikes to school.
John has	**often**	got tasty sandwiches for lunch.

19 Kitty hat am Wochenende viel zu tun. Ordne die Angaben in blau dem richtigen Platz im Satz zu.

1. Kitty ______________ goes swimming ________________ often
2. She ______________ meets her friends ________________ on Saturday
3. She ______________ helps her dad ________________ in his shop
4. She ______________ plays basketball ________________ on Sunday
5. She ______________ walks her dog ________________ in the park
6. She ______________ goes to bed early ________________ never

20 Ben entspannt sich am Wochenende gern. Verbinde die Satzteile zu sinnvollen Sätzen.

Ben never	often stays in bed late.
In the morning he reads	come to his house in the afternoon.
On Sunday he	a good book in his shed in the garden.
His friends usually	television in the evening.
He always watches	goes swimming on Saturday.

21 Ellens Familie treibt gern Sport. Bilde aus den Wörtern vollständige Sätze.

always – Thursday – Ellen – plays – on – tennis

____

every – runs – brother – school – Ellen's – day – to

____

usually – at – go – Ellen's – weekend – parents – swimming – the

____

often – in – on – the – play – they – Sunday – football – park – afternoon

____

in – on – the – Sunday – living – they – always – television – room – watch

____

always – football – watch – they

____

Die Demonstrativpronomen *this/that* und *these/those*

Wenn etwas in der Nähe ist:	Wenn etwas weiter weg ist:
This is my pen **here.**	**That** is my sister in the park.
These are my CDs.	**Those** are my friends over **there.**

22 *This, that, these* oder *those?* Ergänze!

_______________ is my house over there.

_______________ are Henry's cards here.

_______________ is your bag here.

_______________ are my pencils over there.

23 Schau die Bilder an, dann füge *this, that, these* oder *those* ein.

1.

_______________ are my drums here.

2.

_______________'s Kim's football.

3.

_______________ is Pete's dog.

4.

_______________ are your books.

Information heraussuchen

24 Pete und Jenny wollen am Wochenende Tennis spielen. Lies den Dialog und die Aussagen darunter, dann entscheide dich für „richtig“ oder „falsch“.

Pete: Let's play tennis this weekend.
Jenny: That's a good idea. How about Friday evening?
Pete: No, I can't on Friday evening. I always go swimming. How about Saturday morning?
Jenny: OK. At 9 o'clock?
Pete: 9 o'clock? I never get up early on Saturday morning. How about 11 o'clock?
Jenny: No, I can't. I always go to my grandma's house for lunch on Saturday.
Pete: OK. How about Sunday afternoon?
Jenny: No, I always play football in the park on Sunday afternoon. Oh, I've got an idea. You can play football with me and my friends.
Pete: OK. Great. What time?
Jenny: At 2 o'clock.
Pete: OK. See you there then.

1. Jenny hasn't got time on Friday evening. ____________
2. Pete always goes swimming on Friday evening. ____________
3. Pete sometimes gets up early on Saturdays. ____________
4. Jenny can play tennis on Saturday morning. ____________
5. Jenny has lunch at her grandma's on Saturdays. ____________
6. Pete always plays football in the park on Sundays. ____________
7. Jenny and Pete can meet on Sunday afternoon. ____________
8. Jenny and Pete can't play tennis at the weekend. ____________

Das Wesentliche verstehen

25 Lies das Gedicht über Kates Lieblingstag und stelle die Zeilen in die richtige Reihenfolge. Die erste Zeile ist schon angegeben.

My favourite day

- ☐ at half past eight.
- ☐ and it's never boring.
- ☐ and, well, that's sometimes fun.
- ☐ Breakfast at nine
- 1 I get up late
- ☐ I watch TV from eight to ten
- ☐ and we're all fine.
- ☐ I meet friends in the morning
- ☐ After lunch I help my mum
- ☐ and then it's time for bed again.

26 Lies die Beschreibung von Kates Woche durch, dann schau dir das Gedicht nochmals an. Entscheide, welcher Tag Kates Lieblingstag ist.

On schooldays Kate gets up at half past seven and walks to school at quarter past eight. She usually gets home at four o'clock and does some homework, but on Fridays she goes to swimming club. On Saturdays and Sundays she gets up at half past eight and then has breakfast. On Saturday morning she rides her bike to the park and meets some friends there. In the afternoon she helps her mum in the house and in the evening she usually watches TV. On Sunday morning she walks the dog and has lunch at her grandma's house. In the afternoon she meets her friends and sometimes they go to the cinema.

Kate's favourite day is ______________________.

Hören und nachsprechen 20

27 Höre dir die Sätze an und sprich sie nach. Welche Laute sind verbunden? Füge Verbindungen wie im Beispielsatz ein.

Fred‿often gets‿up‿at 8‿o'clock.

Fred and his friends sometimes play football in the park.

He usually reads a book in the evening.

Fred has got a cat and a dog.

Fred's cat often chases the dog. They always sleep on his bag.

Zuhören und einordnen 21

28 Lies zunächst die Wörter und ordne sie der richtigen Spalte zu. Überprüfe dann mithilfe der CD deine Antworten.

bathroom **Thursday** **this** **thanks** **together** **there** **those** **the** **brother** **thirteen** **thirty** **three**

[θ]	[ð]
________________	________________
________________	________________
________________	________________
________________	________________
________________	________________
________________	________________

Das Wesentliche verstehen 22

29 Schau dir erst Julies Kalender an. Dann höre dir auf der CD an, was sie erzählt. Über welchen Tag redet sie?

Friday

7.45 – get up
8.30 – meet Ann and go to school
12.00 – basketball
15.30 – orchestra
18.00 – cinema
21.00 – bed

Saturday

7.45 – get up
8.00 – walk dog
8.30 – go to town
12.00 – go swimming
15.15 – meet band
18.00 – Liz comes to my house
21.30 – bed

Sunday

8.30 – get up
9.00 – go to park
12.00 – lunch at home
15.00 – meet friends in town
18.00 – TV
20.45 – bed

Julie talks about ______________________.

Informationen heraussuchen 23

30 Sandra und Steven wollen sich treffen. Höre dir die CD an und prüfe die Aussagen: richtig oder falsch?

1. Es geht Steven gut. ______________
2. Sandra wohnt in Cardiff. ______________
3. Steven und Sandra möchten Basketball spielen. ______________
4. Steven hat am Freitagabend ein Basketballspiel. ______________
5. Sandra spielt ab 17.30 Uhr im Orchester. ______________
6. Sie möchten sich um 17.30 Uhr treffen und dann zusammen essen. ______________

Revision A (Unit 1 – 3)

Das Alphabet und der unbestimmte Artikel 24

1 Was befindet sich alles im Rucksack? Höre dir die CD an und schreibe die Gegenstände auf. Ergänze dann den richtigen unbestimmten Artikel.

1. ________ ______________________	6. ________ ______________________
2. ________ ______________________	7. ________ ______________________
3. ________ ______________________	8. ________ ______________________
4. ________ ______________________	9. ________ ______________________
5. ________ ______________________	10. ________ ______________________

Zahlen und die Uhrzeit 25

2 Höre dir an, welche Uhrzeiten gesprochen werden, und zeichne sie auf den Uhren ein.

1. 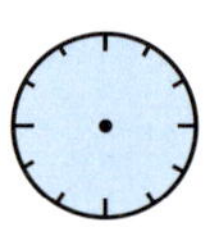	2. 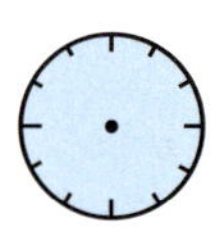	3. 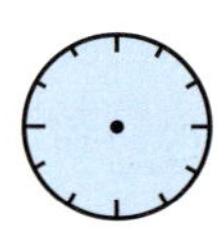	4. 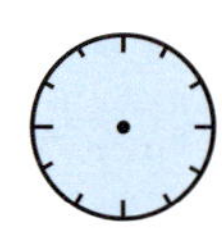
5. 	6. 	7. 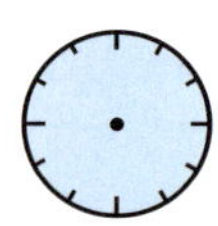	8. 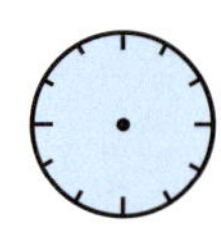
9. 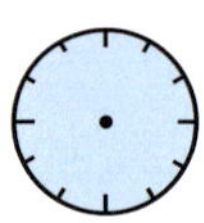	10. 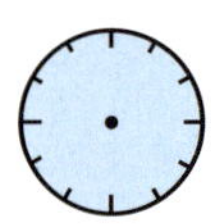	11. 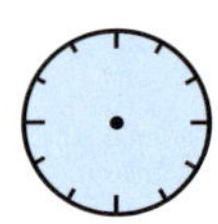	12. 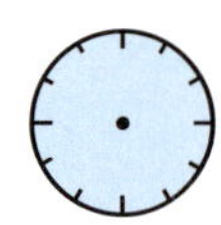

Schule und Familie

3 Sortiere die Wörter, die du in der Buchstabenschlange findest, unter der passenden Überschrift ein und übersetze sie.

family	school

Adjektive

4 Überlege, wie das Gegenteil der genannten Adjektive lautet.

new	_ _ _	great	_ _ _ _ _ _ _ _
big	_ _ _ _ _	right	_ _ _ _ _
short	_ _ _ _	funny	_ _ _ _ _ _
early	_ _ _ _		

Verben: Schule und Hobbys

5 Bilde aus den Wortteilen ganze Verben und schreibe sie in die Lücken.

d	le	ha	ta	lis	pl	ri	spe
ve	ay	ke	ll	de	arn	o	ten

to ______________ a bike

to ______________ a party

to ______________ cards

to ______________ to a CD

to ______________ a word

to ______________ your homework

to ______________ by heart

to ______________ turns

Satzstruktur

6 Bilde ganze Sätze aus den Wörtern. Aufgepasst: Manche sind Fragen!

always – he – his – in – is – shed

____

football – bedroom – don't – play – your – in

____

have – what – that – got – bag – you – in – ?

____

she – her – room – not – got – has – own

____

can – help – I – kitchen – you – in – the – ?

____

often – evening – cards – we – the – play – in

____

Fragen und Antworten

7 Tim stellt seinem Lehrer Fragen. Verbinde die Fragen mit den korrekten Antworten.

What's your name?	It's at home.
How old are you?	It's your homework.
Can you play the drums?	Bristol.
Where are you from?	Yes, I have.
What's this?	That's the caretaker.
Have you got a dog?	Yes, I can.
Where is your dog?	Yes, you are.
Who is that?	Mr Johnson.
Am I late?	21.

Die einfache Gegenwart

8 Ergänze die Verben in der richtigen Form.

to be (2x!) – to run – to get up – to start – to make – to eat – to go (2x!) – to wash – to find – to say – to take

I ________________ at 7.45. I ___________ late. School ________________ at 8.30. I _____________ my face and then I ______________ breakfast. I ________________ my breakfast into the living room and then _____________ upstairs. I can't ________________ my bag. My dog ________________ my breakfast. I _______________ to school. It ___________ 8.35. Oh no. I go into the classroom and _____________, "OK boys and girls. We can start now."

Leseverstehen

9 Lies den Text über die Katze Tom und dann beantworte die Fragen mit „richtig“ oder „falsch“.

I always have breakfast with Kate at eight. She gives me milk and cat food and then goes to school. Sometimes I go with her to school and sometimes I play with Toby in the living room. Toby is a dog and he is very silly. When I eat his breakfast, he chases me. I run and sit on top of the cupboard in the living room. He runs, too, but he can't stop and so he runs into the cupboard. It is very funny.
In the afternoon I usually sleep near the window of the living room and when Kate comes home, we play together. At night I go into the garden and meet my friends. We often sing together – our families like that.

1. Tom frühstückt mit Kate um acht Uhr. ____________
2. Tom geht immer mit Kate zur Schule. ____________
3. Toby kann Tom erwischen. ____________
4. Tom spielt den ganzen Nachmittag mit Kate. ____________
5. Nachts singt Tom zusammen mit seinen Freunden. ____________

Einen Dialog zusammenbauen

10 Lies die Sätze durch, dann ordne sie neu, indem du Ziffern in der richtigen Reihenfolge in die Kästchen einträgst. Wie ergibt sich ein sinnvoller Dialog?

- ☐ We've got a game on Saturday afternoon and Alan can't play.
- ☐ OK. Great. See you then.
- ☐ You're OK. And have you got a ball?
- ☐ Hi Brian. It's Tim here. How are you?
- ☐ Fine. Can you play football at the weekend?
- ☐ See you.
- ☐ Oh, but you know, I'm not good at football.
- ☐ Yes, I have. I can bring it with me.
- ☐ Hi Tim. I'm fine. And you?
- ☐ Yes, I can. Why?

Hörverständnis 26

11 Jill trifft im Kochklub einen neuen Jungen. Höre die CD an und beantworte anschließend die Fragen mit „richtig“ oder „falsch“.

1. Henry wohnt in Cardiff. ____________________
2. Henry ist neu in Bristol. ____________________
3. In Bristol kann man ins Kino gehen. ____________________
4. Henrys Mutter, Vater und Schwester sind auch in Bristol. ____________________
5. Jill trifft ihre Freunde immer um 2 Uhr am Kino. ____________________
6. Henry denkt, er sei im Computerklub. ____________________

Schreiben

12 Schau dir die Bilder an. Was macht Peter am Samstag?

____

____

____

____

Unit 4

Die Stadt

1 Ein Rätsel. Die farbig hinterlegten Kästchen ergeben den Namen eines berühmten Segelschiffes.

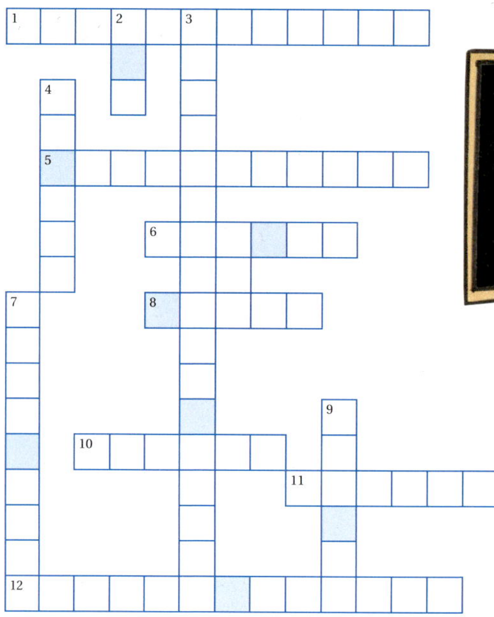

1. You can go swimming here. (2 words)
2. You look at this when you want to know where a place is.
3. You go here when you want to ask questions about a town. (2 words)
4. A lot of people go here on Sundays.
5. You can take this when you want to go places.
6. This is an old place. Tourists often visit it.
7. You can go here when you want to eat chocolate or crisps. (2 words)
8. Boats go on here.
9. You can get lots of things here. It's usually outside.
10. You go here when you want to look at old and interesting things.
11. When you want to cross a river, you can use this.
12. The police work here. (2 words)

Lösungswort: _ _ _ _ y _ _ _ _

Nach dem Weg fragen

2 Schau dir das Bild an und schreibe das richtige Wort oder die richtigen Wörter in die Lücken.

Excuse me. Where's the church? – It's ____________________ the café.

Is the café ____________________ the castle? – Yes, it is.

How can I get to the church? – _________________ Castle Road and then _________________ into Mouse Road and the church is ____________________.

Where's the sweet shop, please? – It's __________________ the police station.

Can I ____________________ the bus to the café? – Yes, you can. There's the bus stop.

How can I get to the sweet shop, please? – ____________________ Castle Road and then ____________________ into Mouse Road. The sweet shop is ____________________

Wichtige Ausdrücke

3 Vervollständige die folgenden Ausdrücke.

E _ _ _ _ _ _ _. Where's the police station, please?

I'm sorry. I d _ _ ' _ k _ _ _.

The castle is in Orinoco Road. It's opposite the café and next to a museum.

Er sorry, but c _ _ y _ _ r _ _ _ _ _ t _ _ _, p _ _ _ _ _?

C _ _ I a _ _ y _ _ _ q _ _ _ _ _ _ _?

Yes, of course.

H _ _ c _ _ _ g _ _ _ _ t _ _ river?

You can walk there or you can take the bus.

When does the bus go?

There are buses e _ _ _ _ twenty m _ _ _ _ _ _.

Himmelsrichtungen

4 Wie heißen die Himmelsrichtungen? Ergänze.

_ _ r _ _

_ e _ _

_ _ _ _

_ _ _ _ _

Verben

5 Ordne die durcheinandergeratenen Buchstaben zu Verben der Fortbewegung und übersetze sie.

to aisl ______________ ______________

to hrruy pu ______________ ______________

to accth ______________ (a train) (einen Zug)______________

to deirv ______________ ______________

to akpr ______________ ______________

6 Finde sechs Verben, die mit Sprechen zu tun haben, und schreibe sie in die passenden Sätze. Vorsicht: Ein Verb besteht aus zwei Wörtern!

I want to ______________ some information.

Can you ______________ that, please?

I ______________ the café is near here.

What does GMT ______________?

What do you ______________ that place?

Can you ______________ how many people live here?

7 Diese Verben brauchst du für Dinge, die man in der Schule tut.

arbeiten ______________ aufschreiben ______________

korrigieren ______________ kämpfen ☺ ______________

Die Objektformen der Personalpronomen

Subjektform	Objektform	
I	Give **me** my ball, please.	mich/mir
you	I can see **you.**	dich/dir
he	I can help **him.**	ihn/ihm
she	You can't talk to **her** now.	sie/ihr
it	Can you give **it** to Jane, please?	ihm/ihn/es/sie
we	Dad always takes **us** to school.	uns
you	Can I play with **you,** please?	euch
they	Mrs Smith teaches **them** English.	ihnen/sie

8 Ein Tag in London. Schreibe die richtige Objektform in die Lücken.

Buckingham Palace? Oh yes. I want to visit ______________.

Which funny girls? I can't see ______________.

There's a man. Let's ask ______________.

What about Gemma? Let's get ______________ a present.

Let's take a taxi. Excuse me. Can you take ______________ to the Thames Barrier, please?

9 Schreibe die richtige Objekt- oder Subjektform in die Lücken.

Hello. __________'m a taxi driver and I can show __________ everywhere in London. Come with __________ and listen. Do you know Madonna? Well, that's her house. I often see __________ in the garden. Lots of tourists want to see her house and I often bring __________ in my taxi. I don't think __________ likes that. And do you know Robbie Williams? There's his house. Can you see __________ behind the trees? I don't like __________, but his songs are great. What do you think?

Verneinte Aussagen mit *don't*

Wenn du einen Satz verneinen willst, der ein Hilfsverb wie *can* oder *have got* oder eine Form von *to be* enthält, hängst du einfach *not* an. Steht das Vollverb aber allein, gebrauchst du das Hilfsverb *don't (do not)* vor dem Vollverb:

I **eat** chocolate.	I **don't eat** mice.
You **play** football.	But you **don't play** the drums.
We **get up** early on Monday.	We **don't get up** early on Saturday.
Rob and Ann **know** Sally.	They **don't know** her brother.

10 Sally redet Unsinn. Lies, was sie behauptet, und setze ihre Aussagen in die verneinte Form.

____

____

____

____

11 Rob widerspricht Sallys Aussagen. Schreibe auf, was er ihr antwortet.

I play football every weekend. No, you don't ______________________

I am good at football. ______________________

I can play the guitar. ______________________

I have got a lot of friends. ______________________

I do my homework. ______________________

Pete and Fred like me. ______________________

Entscheidungsfragen und Kurzantworten mit *do*

Wenn du kein Hilfsverb hast, stellst du *do* an den Satzanfang:

Aussage	**Frage**	**Kurzantwort**
I **like** chocolate.	**Do** you **like** chocolate?	Yes, I **do.**
We often **play** tennis.	**Do** you **play** cards?	No, we **don't.**
They **live** in London.	**Do** they **live** near you?	Yes, they **do.**

Wenn du eine Frage mit Hilfsverb oder mit *to be* bilden willst, stellst du einfach das Hilfsverb oder *am/are/is* vor das Subjekt:

Aussage	**Frage**	**Kurzantwort**
I **can play** tennis.	**Can** you **play** tennis?	No, I **can't.**
I'**ve got** a sister.	**Have** you **got** a sister?	Yes, I **have.**
I **am** 11.	**Are** you 11?	No, **I'm not.**

12 In Greenwich Park. Bilde aus den angegebenen Wörtern Fragen.

do – Greenwich – Park – like – you – ?

___

you – park – do – near – live – the – ?

___

visit – do – often – Cutty Sark – tourists – the – ?

___

people – Thames – do – walk – under – the – ?

___

Underground – Canary Wharf – to – do – take – we – the – ?

___

13 Ein Interview mit einem Spaziergänger in Greenwich Park. Ergänze die fehlenden Wörter.

__________ you __________ here? – No, I __________. I live in west London.

__________ you often __________ here? – Yes, I __________. I come here every week. My parents live near here.

__________ they like it here? – Yes, ____________________.

_______________ drive here? – No, I __________. I take the Underground.

14 Lies die Ergebnisse eines Projekts über Greenwich Park und formuliere die Fragen und Kurzantworten dazu.

Some boys come here with their skateboards every week.
You can see the Thames from Greenwich Park.
One museum has got a lot of old clocks.
A lot of tourists come here in summer.
Some people have lunch in the café.

Do some boys ____?

– Yes, ____________________

____

– ____________________

____

– ____________________

____

– ____________________

____

– ____________________

Fragen und verneinte Aussagen mit *does* und *doesn't*

Mit *he, she* und *it* verwendest du *does* und *doesn't* statt *do* und *don't*:

bejahte Aussage	**verneinte Aussage**
She **watches** TV.	She **doesn't** watch TV.
He **does** his homework at home.	He **doesn't** do his homework.
Entscheidungsfrage	**Kurzantwort**
Does she go swimming on Saturday?	Yes, she **does.**
Does Tom know your sister?	No, he **doesn't.**
Does Ann like chocolate?	Yes, she **does** but she **doesn't** like cheese.

15 Zoe hat eine Freundin, Glenda. Die beiden sind sich gar nicht ähnlich. Formuliere verneinte Aussagen über Glenda.

Zoe lives in Greenwich.

____

Zoe watches football on TV.

____

Zoe goes to museums.

____

Zoe reads books in the evening.

____

16 Lies die Informationen über Jean durch, die in der Nähe von Greenwich Park wohnt. Dann bilde Fragen und die passenden Kurzantworten.

lives near Greenwich Park	☑
comes from Italy	☑
likes English food	☒
goes to the park with her skateboard	☑

____

____

____

____

17 Ein Gespräch mit David über seine Oma. Ergänze die fehlenden Wörter.

Hello. Your grandma comes from Italy. ___________ she speak Italian to you?

Yes, she ___________, but she speaks English, too.

___________ she like England?

Yes, she ___________, but she ___________ like English food.

___________ she often go to the park?

Yes, she ___________. She ___________ there with her skateboard.

And ___________ she go fast?

No, she ___________ and it looks very funny because she always listens to her discman on her skateboard.

18 Skateboards. Verbinde die Fragen und die Kurzantworten mit einer Linie.

Have you got a skateboard?	No, I don't.
Does it go fast?	Yes, I can.
Is there a place for skateboards near you?	No, they don't.
Can you use it in the park?	Yes, it does.
Do your parents like it?	No, there isn't.
Do you take it to school?	Yes, I have.

19 Wie kommst du hin? Bilde Fragen und Aussagen aus den angegebenen Wörtern und verwende die richtige Form des Verbs.

you – to go – to school – by bus – ?

____

my mum – to take – me – to school

____

your dad – to take – the Underground – to work – ?

____

my dad – not – to go – by Underground

____

your friends – to walk – to school – ?

____

my friends – not – to walk – to school

____

Fragen mit Fragewörtern und *do/does*

Fragewort	**Hilfsverb**	**Subjekt**	**Vollverb**		**Antwort**
What	does	Lisa	play	in the evening?	Cards.
When	does	John	get up?		At 7.45.
Where	do	they	go	at the weekend?	To town.
Why	don't	you	like	it?	Because …
How	do	you	get	to school?	By bus.

20 Eine Umfrage im Park. Formuliere Fragen, indem du nach dem Satzteil fragst, der unterstrichen ist.

1. When ____ ?

   The café opens at <u>10 o'clock</u>.

2. ____

   I get here <u>by bus</u>.

3. ____

   I meet <u>my friends</u>.

4. ____

   I <u>play football</u>.

5. ____

   We play football <u>near the playground</u>.

6. ____

   My dog likes it here <u>because</u> he can chase the birds.

Informationen heraussuchen

21 Lies den Text durch und beantworte anschließend die Fragen.

I live in Durham. It's a small town and it's very old. Tourists often come here because it's very beautiful, too. There's a river in the centre of town and you can cross it on one of the bridges. When it's warm, people sometimes jump *(springen)* into the river from the bridges and swim in it. That's great fun. You can walk by the river, too, and a lot of people go by boat on the river. Big ships don't come down the river because it is only a small river. There's a castle and a cathedral in the centre of Durham near the river. They look beautiful and people live in the castle. Watch a Harry Potter film and you can see part of the cathedral.
There are also interesting museums and shops in Durham. You can do a lot of things in Durham and the sea is near, too. Durham is in the north of England but it's easy to get there. You can get there by train in about two hours from London.

1. Is Durham a big town? – ______________________
2. Why do tourists go there? – ______________________
3. How can you cross the river? – ______________________
4. What do people do in the river? – ______________________
5. Do big ships go down the river? Why? Why not? – ______________________

   ____
6. What can you visit in the centre of Durham? – ______________________

   ____
7. Is there a big church in Durham? – ______________________
8. What can you see in a Harry Potter film? – ______________________
9. How can you get to London from Durham? – ______________________
10. How many hours is it from London to Durham by train? – ______________________

Das Wesentliche verstehen

22 Lies den Text und stelle die Blöcke in die richtige Reihenfolge.

A
There are lots of interesting things there – old things and places where other people don't go. One day Glen finds an old tunnel and wants to look at it with Robert.
"Let's visit that old tunnel," says Glen.
"Where is it?" says Robert. "We haven't got a lot of time today."

B
"Oh no. There are people in here. Let's go back," says Robert. Then they hear a train. They go back to the wall and wait. Then they hear the woman. She shouts, "Help!" What can they do? They can't see a thing. The train doesn't go past but it's quiet again. They walk out of the tunnel. They don't say anything but they are not happy. Then Robert finds an old magazine from April 1982. They read, "Woman falls in front of train."

C
Glen and Robert live in London. They're new there and they are friends. Glen comes from Cardiff and Robert comes from Bristol. They go to the same school and they're in the same class. After school they often explore *(erforschen)* the part of London near their houses.

D
"But it's only a tunnel," says Glen, "And trains don't come here now because there are new tunnels under London. Come on. Let's go in."
They go in and walk down the tunnel. They can't see a lot because it's so dark *(dunkel)*. It's very scary. Then they hear a man and a woman.

E
"It's near the river," says Glen, "and it looks very scary."
"OK," says Robert, "Let's go."
They walk to the river and Glen can't find the tunnel at first. It's behind some trees. After about five minutes he finds it and shows it to Robert.
"I don't want to go in there. It's too scary," Robert says.

Richtige Reihenfolge: ______________________________

Hören und zuordnen 27

23 [w] oder [v]? Höre dir die CD an und ordne die Wörter der richtigen Spalte zu.

[w]	[v]
______________	______________
______________	______________
______________	______________
______________	______________
______________	______________

Ein Dialog 28

24 Lisa besucht ihren Cousin Ryan in London. Finde heraus, in welcher Reihenfolge der Dialog stehen muss. Überprüfe deine Antwort mithilfe der CD.

A ☐ *Lisa:* Who do you watch?

B ☐ *Lisa:* And what do you do there?

C ☐ *Lisa:* And what do you do in Covent Garden? Look at the flowers?

D ☐ *Lisa:* What do you usually do on a Saturday?

E ☐ *Lisa:* No, I don't.

F ☐ *Ryan:* Well, I often go to Covent Garden or look at the shops.

G ☐ *Ryan:* No. Don't you know Covent Garden?

H ☐ *Ryan:* Well, people sing there and it's always fun to watch the tourists.

I ☐ *Ryan:* Well, let's go there tomorrow. It's great. You can watch people there.

J ☐ *Ryan:* I usually go to the centre of London.

Informationen heraussuchen 29

25 Höre dir die CD an: Es wird nach vier Gebäuden gefragt. Beschrifte die Gebäude entsprechend!

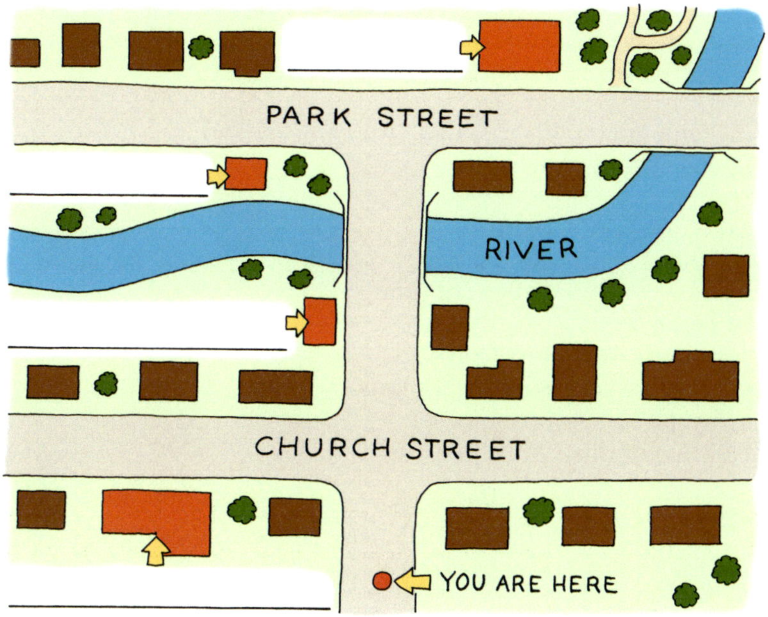

Zuhören und verstehen 30

26 James ist neu in der Stadt. Höre dir die CD an und beantworte dann die Fragen dazu.

1. Where's the swimming pool? – ______________________________
2. Is the swimming pool next to the church? – ______________________
3. What time does the swimming pool open? – ______________________
4. Why is James not happy? – ______________________________
5. Where does Mr Gore say that James can go swimming? – ____________
6. Does he want to go swimming there? – __________________________

Unit 5

Einkaufen

1 Trage die fehlenden Wörter in das Gitter ein. Die farbigen Kästchen ergeben das Lösungswort.

1. What ... are you? – Large.
2. Sweatshirts and T-shirts are ... .
3. You need ... when you go shopping.
4. That pen is 32 ... .
5. Five pounds for a pen? That's ... .
6. What size are you? Small, ... or large?
7. Can I ... on this T-shirt, please?
8. Have you got this T-shirt in extra ... ?

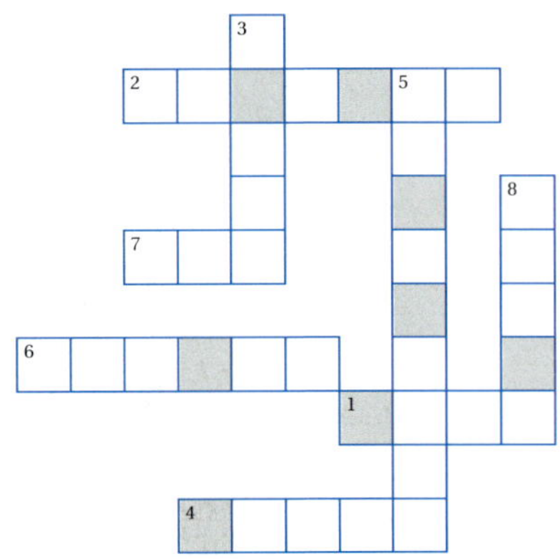

Lösungswort: ____________________

2 Vervollständige Frage und Antwort mit den angegebenen Ausdrücken.

I'd like to try on – How much is this pen, please? – Excuse me, do you sell – Yes, here you are.

Excuse me. Have you got this T-shirt in medium? –

____

____ – It's two pounds fifty.

____________________________________ sweatshirts? – Yes, they're over there.

____ these sweatshirts, please.

– OK, but you can only take three things with you.

Die Monate

3 Trage die Monate auf Englisch in die Lücken ein.

Januar	____________	Juli	____________
Februar	____________	August	____________
März	____________	September	____________
April	____________	Oktober	____________
Mai	____________	November	____________
Juni	____________	Dezember	____________

Das Datum 31

4 Höre dir die CD an und schreibe das genannte Datum auf.

1. ____________	8. ____________
2. ____________	9. ____________
3. ____________	10. ____________
4. ____________	11. ____________
5. ____________	12. ____________
6. ____________	13. ____________
7. ____________	14. ____________

Geburtstag

5 Finde acht Wörter, die mit Geburtstagspartys zu tun haben, und übersetze sie.

_______________ – _______________

_______________ – _______________

_______________ – _______________

_______________ – _______________

_______________ – _______________

_______________ – _______________

_______________ – _______________

_______________ – _______________

e	x	c	i	t	e	d
d	c	a	n	d	l	e
w	s	i	v	p	k	n
e	j	l	i	v	m	s
p	a	r	t	y	b	u
r	g	c	a	k	e	r
e	e	f	t	u	z	p
s	r	t	i	l	k	r
e	d	h	o	o	o	i
n	r	g	n	u	x	s
t	q	s	y	d	a	e

6 Ordne die Buchstaben in der richtigen Reihenfolge, um vier Verben zu erhalten, die mit Geburtstag zu tun haben.

viinte *to* _______________

caend _______________

ghaul _______________

gins _______________

7 Welche Verben fehlen hier? Ergänze.

I l_ _ _ in London Road.

I'd l_ _ _ to invite you to my party.

I w_ _ _ lots of presents.

Kochen

8 Füge die Wörter an den richtigen Stellen ein.

cake **cook** **count** **eggs**

how much **need** **recipe** **sugar**

Mary: Are you a good ________________?

Chris: Yes, of course. OK. First, let's look for a ________________.

Mary: This looks good. Chocolate ________________.

Chris: OK. Let's make that. What do we ________________?

Mary: We need two ________________, flour and ________________.

Chris: ______________________ sugar do we need?

Mary: Er. 125 grams. And how many eggs have we got?

Chris: I don't know. Let's ________________ them.

9 Was brauchst du? Streiche das falsche Wort durch.

I want to buy a bag of flour/eggs.

We need a cup of crisps/water.

Have we got a box of sugar/eggs?

I want to eat lots of/many pizza.

Let's make a few sandwiches/cake.

We've only got a little sugar/eggs.

Want to und *would like to* + Infinitiv

Nach *want* und *would like* steht immer ***to*** und der **Infinitiv**:

What do you want to eat?	Was willst du essen?
I want to eat sandwiches.	Ich will Sandwiches essen.
Sally doesn't want to eat cake.	Sally will keinen Kuchen essen.
Would you like to have a party?	Möchtest du ein Fest machen?
I'd like to invite lots of friends.	Ich möchte viele Freunde einladen.

10 Stelle diese Wörter um, sodass sie sinnvolle Sätze ergeben.

chocolate cake – you – would – make – to – a – like – ?

____

of – want – I – chocolate crispies – lots – eat – to

____

you – buy – sandwich – to – do – want – a – ?

____

don't – eat – I – want – cheese sandwiches – to

____

11 Eine Freundin von dir will Geburtstag feiern. Übersetze.

Wann möchte sie das Fest machen?

____

Wen will sie einladen?

____

Sie möchte keinen Kuchen backen.

____

Die Ordnungszahlen

Um eine Ordnungszahl zu bilden, hängst du einfach *th* an die Grundzahl:
4th = the fourth – 17th = the seventeenth – 25th = the twenty-fifth
Bei 1, 2 und 3 gibt es Ausnahmen:
1st = the **first** – 2nd = the **second** – 3rd = the **third**
Bei diesen Ordnungszahlen ändert sich die Schreibweise:
fi**ve:** 5th = the fi**fth** – eigh**t:** 8th = the eigh**th** – nin**e:** 9th = the nin**th** – twel**ve:** 12th = the twel**fth**
Bei den Ordnungszahlen *20th* bis *90th* wird das *y* zu *ie*:
twent**y:** 20th = the twent**ie**th – thirt**y:** 30th = the thirtieth – fort**y:** 40th = the fort**ie**th

12 Schreibe die Ordnungszahlen aus.

7th ____________________ 9th ____________________

12th ____________________ 2nd ____________________

21st ____________________ 32nd ____________________

Das Datum schreiben

Es gibt zwei Möglichkeiten, das Datum zu schreiben und auszusprechen.

Man schreibt:		Man spricht:
18th January	→	"the eighteenth **of** January"
January 18th	→	"January the eighteenth"

13 Schreibe diese Daten so aus, wie man sie sprechen kann – auf beide Arten.

10.5. ____________________ / ____________________

31.10. ____________________ / ____________________

12.3. ____________________ / ____________________

2.8. ____________________ / ____________________

Die Verlaufsform der Gegenwart

Mit der Verlaufsform der Gegenwart drückst du aus, was jemand gerade macht. Es wird mit einer Form von *to be* + Vollverb + *-ing* gebildet:

I **am watching** TV.
You **are playing** tennis.
He/She **is reading** a book.
It **is eating** cheese.
We **are having** a party.
You **are making** a cake.
They **are doing** their homework.

Bei der Verneinung steht *not* vor der *-ing*-Form des Verbs:
I **am not eating** the cake.

14 Sieh dir die Bilder an und beschreibe, was geschieht.

1.

A man ______ his dog.

2.

The dogs ______ a ball.

3.

She ______

4.

You ______ on a sofa.

5.

We ______

6.

I ______ a cake.

Fragen und Kurzantworten in der Verlaufsform

Bei Fragen ohne Fragewort rückt die Form von *to be* an den Satzanfang. In der Kurzantwort wird nur die Form von *to be* wiederaufgegriffen.

Are you talking to Gemma?	Yes, **I am.**
Is Tony sleeping?	Yes, he **is.**
Are you two watching TV?	No, we **aren't.**
Are they having a good time?	Yes, they **are.**

15 Bilde aus den Wörtern Fragesätze in der Verlaufsform.

you – to make – a cup of tea – ? ____________________

they – to dance – ? ____________________

he – to try on – that sweatshirt – ? ____________________

we – to sing – the right song – ? ____________________

I – to walk – the right way – ? ____________________

she – to eat – breakfast – ? ____________________

16 Auf einem Fest. Beantworte die Fragen mit einer Kurzantwort.

Is Christine dancing with Pete? Yes, ____________________

Are Alan and Robert watching TV? Yes, ____________________

Are you eating all the cake? No, ____________________

Are we having a good time? Yes, ____________________

Is Kyle laughing at me? No, ____________________

Is Jane waiting for me? Yes, ____________________

17 Susanne feiert Geburtstag. Ergänze die richtige Form des Verbs.

Susanne usually goes swimming on Saturday afternoon but today she (not/to swim) ____________________. She (to have) _______________ a birthday party in the garden. What (the children/to do) _______________ _______________ at her party? The girls (to play) _______________ a game under a tree and the boys (to eat) _______________. (Susanne/to have) ____________________ a good time? Yes, _______________. (her parents/to help) ______________________________ at the party? No, _______________. But they (to watch) _______________ __________ the birthday party.

Was passiert? 32

18 Höre dir die CD an und beantworte dann die Fragen mit einer Kurzantwort. Lautet deine Antwort nein, formuliere, was tatsächlich geschieht.

1. Are they playing football? – ______________________________
____
2. Is she doing her homework? – ______________________________
____
3. Are they dancing? – ______________________________
____
4. Am I riding my bike? – ______________________________
____

Die Mengenwörter *much/many* und *a little/a few*

Du verwendest ***a little*** und ***much*** bei Nomen im Singular, die nicht zählbar sind: *flour, water, cheese*.
A few und ***many*** stehen bei Nomen im Plural, die zählbar sind.

How **much** water do we need?	Wie **viel** Wasser brauchen wir?
How **many** tins have we got?	Wie **viele** Dosen haben wir?
I need **a little** sugar.	Ich brauche **ein wenig** Zucker.
And **a few** eggs.	Und **ein paar** Eier.

19 Welche dieser Nomen sind zählbar, welche unzählbar?

birthday – box – flour – help – homework – street – tea – year

zählbar: ______________________________

unzählbar: ______________________________

20 Liam und seine Mutter kaufen ein. Ergänze *much, many, a little* oder *a few*.

Mum: Come on. We haven't got ____________ time. What do we need?

Liam: Er, we haven't got ____________ flour. And we haven't got ____________ eggs.

Mum: Well, we only need ____________ eggs and ____________ flour so that's OK.

Liam: Have we got ____________ chocolate? We need a lot or we can't make ____________ chocolate crispies.

Mum: Yes, but we only need ____________ chocolate cripsies because nobody likes them.

Liam: What? But … Oh, I see, it was a joke.

Mengen mit *of*

a box **of** eggs	eine Schachtel Eier
two tins **of** dog food	zwei Dosen Hundefutter
a pound **of** flour	ein Pfund Mehl
two bags **of** sugar	zwei Tüten Zucker
a cup **of** water	eine Tasse Wasser

21 Was siehst du?

1. ______________ 2. ______________ 3. ______________

4. ______________ 5. ______________ 6. ______________

22 Was braucht diese Hexe zum Kochen? Übersetze.

______________ eine Tüte Mäuse

______________ zwei Dosen Sand *(sand)*

______________ drei Kartons alte Schuhe

______________ ein Pfund Kerzen

Der *of*-Genitiv

Monday is the first **day of the week.**
The **door of the car** is open.
The first **page of the book** isn't here.

Der Genitiv mit *of* entspricht dem *s*-Genitiv: Er drückt aus, dass etwas zu etwas anderem gehört. Man verwendet den Genitiv mit *of* bei Dingen und den *s*-Genitiv bei Menschen oder Tieren.
The **dog's eyes** are green.
The **door of the house** is red.

23 Was gehört wozu? Bilde ganze Sätze. Das erste Wort ist schon angegeben.

find – April – I – a – day – book – on – of – the – first

I ______________________________

a – the – the – there's – first – book – page – house – of – on

There's ______________________________

the – the – door – house – of – opens

The ______________________________

a – the – house – family – photo – of – in – my – is

A ______________________________

24 Der *of*-Genitiv oder der *s*-Genitiv? Übersetze.

die Kleidung des Mädchens ______________________________

der Farbe der Dose ______________________________

die Augen der Katze ______________________________

der erste Tag der zweiten Woche ______________________________

Das Wesentliche verstehen

25 Ein Geburtstagsfest. Schaue dir das Bild an und lies dann die Texte dazu. Welche Beschreibung passt am besten?

A

Today is the 5th March and it's my sister's birthday. She's having a party and all her friends are here. What are they doing now? Well, my sister isn't dancing on the table but her friends are singing on the chairs. Some boys are jumping on the sofa. I don't know why. One boy is playing the drums and some boys are playing football. And what am I doing? I'm taking photos. My parents are in the garden. They're talking to a neighbour and they're not looking into the living room.

B

Today is the 5th May and it's my brother's birthday. He's having a party and all his friends are here. What are they doing now? Well, my brother is dancing on the table and his friends are singing on the chairs. Some boys are jumping on the sofa and the cat is sitting on a cupboard. One boy is playing the drums and some boys are playing football. But they aren't using a football! And what am I doing? I'm taking photos. My parents are in the garden. My mum is talking to a neighbour and my dad is now looking into the living room and his face is getting very red.

C

Today is the 5th March and it's my sister's birthday. She's having a party and all her friends are here. What are they doing now? Well, my sister is dancing on the table and her friends are singing on the chairs. Some boys are jumping on the sofa and the cat is sitting on a cupboard. One boy is playing the drums and some boys are playing football. But they aren't using a football! And what am I doing? I'm taking photos. My parents are in the garden. My mum is talking to a neighbour and my dad is now looking into the living room and his face is getting very red.

→ Beschreibung __________ stimmt mit dem Bild überein.

Informationen heraussuchen

26 Paul sucht ein Geburtstagsgeschenk für seine Schwester. Lies die Geschichte durch und beantworte die Fragen.

It's four o'clock on Monday and I'm in town and I'm looking for a present for my sister. I usually go swimming on Monday after school but I can't today because I need a present. I think she'd like a sweatshirt so I'm going into a clothes shop now.
It's five o'clock now and I still haven't got a present. I'm in my third clothes shop. Oh look, there's a nice pink sweatshirt, but it's £ 15.99.
It's too expensive for me so I go to a book shop. I look for thirty minutes but I can't find a good book. I know. I think she'd like a CD of her favourite band.
It's six o'clock and I'm outside a music shop. It isn't open. It closes at half past five, so I go home with no present. I'm not happy.
"What can I do?" I ask my mum when I get home.
"Well, why don't you get her the CD tomorrow *(morgen)*?" says my mum.
"It's her birthday tomorrow."
"No, it isn't. Her birthday's on the 15th of June and today is the 13th June."
"Oh."

1. Why is Paul in town?

____

2. Does he usually go to town on Mondays?

____

3. How many clothes shops does he go in?

____

4. Why doesn't he buy the sweatshirt?

____

5. Why doesn't he buy a book?

____

6. What time does the music shop close?

____

Hören und wiederholen 33

27 Höre dir die Sätze auf der CD an und sprich sie nach. Geht die Stimme am Ende des Satzes nach oben oder nach unten? Zeichne einen entsprechenden Pfeil in die Kästchen.

Is it Ann's birthday today? ☐

No, it's on the fifteenth of June. ☐

Have you got her a present? ☐

No, I haven't. ☐

What are you doing now? ☐

I'm making a present for Ann. ☐

Hören und Informationen heraussuchen 34

28 Joe möchte sich etwas kaufen. Höre dir den Dialog an und beantworte danach die Fragen.

1. What's Joe looking for? ______________________
2. He finds a nice sweatshirt.
   How much is it? ______________________
3. Which size does he want? ______________________
4. Which sizes have they got? ______________________
5. Which size does he try on? ______________________
6. Does he want to buy it? ______________________
7. Why or why not? ______________________

Hören und schreiben 35

29 In dem kleinen Geschäft ist viel los. Höre dir die CD an, dann schreibe auf, was die genannten Dinge kosten.

chocolate: ______________ green apples: ______________

crisps: ______________ red apples: ______________

dog magazine: ______________ red bags: ______________

Hören und korrigieren 36

30 Zu Emmas Geburtstag ruft ihre Oma *(grandma)* an. Leider ist sie etwas schwerhörig. Danach erzählt sie Emmas Opa *(grandpa)*, was Emma gesagt hat. Schreibe auf, was falsch ist, und ergänze, was Emma wirklich macht.

Grandpa: Well, Grandma. Is Emma having a good time?
Grandma: Yes, she is. She's having a party with all her friends and they're all swimming in the garden.
Grandpa: Swimming in the garden?
Grandma: Yes, and her mum and dad are walking in the park.
Grandpa: Why aren't they at the party?
Grandma: I don't know. Her brother John is playing cards in the bedroom and they've got lots of food, pizzas and sandwiches and chocolate cake.

Revision B (Unit 4 – 5)

Wortschatz – *Odd one out!*

1 Finde das Wort, das nicht zu den anderen passt.

1. eggs – flour – recipe – sugar ____________________
2. to invite – to dance – to laugh – to sing ____________________
3. ship – transport – train – Underground ____________________
4. to ask for – to repeat – to speak – to work ____________________
5. east – north – south – left ____________________
6. department store – market – newsagent – money ____________________

Adjektive

2 Finde sieben Adjektive in dem Wortgitter und ordne sie dem passenden Substantiv zu. Es gibt nur eine Möglichkeit, sie alle unterzubringen.

a ____________________ castle

a ____________________ man

a ____________________ cake

a ____________________ sentence

____________________ transport

an ____________________ question

a ____________________ T-shirt

w	e	o	a	p	q	j
f	a	m	o	u	s	u
d	s	y	f	b	k	m
c	y	m	j	l	a	b
s	p	e	c	i	a	l
h	e	d	g	c	b	e
k	a	i	l	o	r	d
p	s	u	u	b	l	r
i	y	m	r	i	c	h

Die einfache Gegenwart

3 *Mike's family.* Formuliere Fragen zu den angegebenen Antworten, indem du nach den unterstrichenen Satzteilen fragst.

1. ______________________________ – We live in London.
2. ______________________________ – Yes, I do. I like London a lot.
3. ______________________________ – I usually meet my friends in the evening.
4. ______________________________ – My brother often goes to the cinema.

4 Kate möchte Lisa ein Geschenk kaufen. Übersetze den Dialog.

Naomi: Was willst du kaufen? ______________________________

Kate: Ich will ein Buch kaufen. ______________________________

Naomi: Aber Lisa mag keine Bücher. ______________________________

Kate: Ja, aber sie mag Musik und dieses Buch ist über Musik. ______ ______________________________ and this book is about music.

Naomi: Spielt Lisa noch in einer Band? ______________________________

Kate: Ja, aber sie spielt nicht mit ihrer alten Band. Sie hat eine neue Band.______________________________. She's got a new band.

Die Verlaufsform der Gegenwart

5 Ein Tag in der Stadt. Ergänze die Lücken mit den richtigen Verbformen.

Hi Ben. What ______________________________ (you/to do)? – I (to sit) ______________________________ in a café. – (you/to eat) ______________ ___________ your lunch? – No, __________________. I (to read) __________ ____________ a book. – And what (your friends/to do) _________________ _________________? – Well, Kylie (to try on) _________________________ ___________ a sweatshirt in a clothes shop and Mark __________________ __________ (to look) at some CDs. – (they/to look for) _________________ _____________ a present for their mum? – No, they (not/to look for) ______________________________ a present. They haven't got any money.

Die Subjekt- und Objektformen der Personalpronomen

6 Trage die richtige Form der Personalpronomen ein.

Hi. It's ____________, Yvonne. Is Peter there? – Yes, ____________ is. – Can I speak to ____________? – No, ____________ can't because he's talking to Susan on his mobile. – Oh, ________ want to speak to _________, too. – Well, why don't you come here and then you can speak to ____________? You only live up the road.

Zuhören und verstehen 37

7 Jack möchte seinen Geburtstag feiern. Höre dir die CD an und beantworte danach die Fragen.

1. When is Jack's birthday? ______________________

2. Does Jack usually have birthday parties? ______________________

3. Why doesn't he want to have a party at the swimming pool?

____

4. Why doesn't he want to have a party at a pizza place?

____

5. Why does he want to invite Peter?

____

Dialoge zusammenstellen

8 Kochen und Einkaufen. Ordne die Sätze zu zwei verschiedenen Dialogen und beschrifte sie jeweils mit A1 bis A4 und mit B1 bis B4.

[A1] Excuse me. Have you got the new 4U CD?

[ ] Oh, we only need a little.

[ ] It's 10.50.

[ ] Well, we've got eggs, flour and sugar, but how much chocolate do we need?

[ ] OK. Have we got everything for the chocolate cake?

[ ] Yes, we have. It's over there under the big poster.

[ ] Oh, thank you. How much is it?

[ ] What? I'm sure we need lots of chocolate.

Übersetzen

9 Übersetze den kleinen Text.

Emma möchte einen Kuchen backen, aber sie hat nur ein bisschen Mehl und ein paar Eier. Sie geht einkaufen, aber die Läden sind nicht offen. Warum? Es ist halb vier morgens und Emma schläft noch.

____

____

____

____

Bilder beschreiben

10 Sieh dir das Bild an und beschreibe, was du siehst.

____

____

____

____

____

____

Unit 6

Im Urlaub

1 Ein Gedicht. Ergänze die passenden Wörter.

address book – arcade games – hear – holiday – ice-cream – pier – post-cards – rocks – sand

Every year we like to go away

for a week or two's ______________________.

I like to sit upon the ______________________

with an ______________________ in my hand.

I always go to the mile long ______________________

and play ______________________ and often ______________________

the sound of waves upon the ______________________

and see people playing with their dogs.

And then it's time for me to look

for my little old ______________________

because before my holiday ends

I must write ________________ to my friends.

2 Was macht man im Urlaub? Finde die passenden Verben.

You can … _ _ _ a kite. _ _ _ a boat. _ _ _ _ your bags.

_ _ _ _ _ a mountain. _ _ _ _ _ _ _ _ _ on the sea. _ _ _ _ _ a sand castle.

3 Finde die sieben versteckten Wörter in dem Wortgitter und übersetze sie.

w	c	a	q	y	b	l	k
m	o	u	n	t	a	i	n
f	a	o	m	h	e	g	o
j	s	p	s	z	f	h	h
n	t	i	e	k	g	t	a
o	c	e	a	n	l	h	r
m	d	u	s	u	m	o	b
c	s	v	i	z	i	u	o
a	y	d	d	i	l	s	u
f	d	c	e	k	s	e	r
v	i	l	l	a	g	e	o

__________ – __________ __________ – __________

__________ – __________ __________ – __________

__________ – __________ __________ – __________

__________ – __________

Zwei-Wort-Verben

4 Welches Wort fehlt nach dem Verb? Ergänze.

What do you think __________ Penzance?

I need to look __________ that word in my dictionary.

I'm waiting __________ Ann again.

Can you take __________ your wellies before you go into the house, please?

I often read __________ my little sister.

Click __________ the picture for more information.

I'd like to get __________ the boat and sail to France.

Jahreszeiten

5 Übersetze die folgenden Wörter.

Jahreszeit ______________________________

Winter ______________________________

Frühling ______________________________

Sommer ______________________________

Herbst ______________________________

Das Wetter

6 Suche die acht Wörter heraus, die sich in der Buchstabenschlange verbergen und mit dem Wetter zu tun haben, und schreibe sie in die richtige Lücke. Vorsicht: Bei einem Wort brauchst du noch einen Bindestrich!

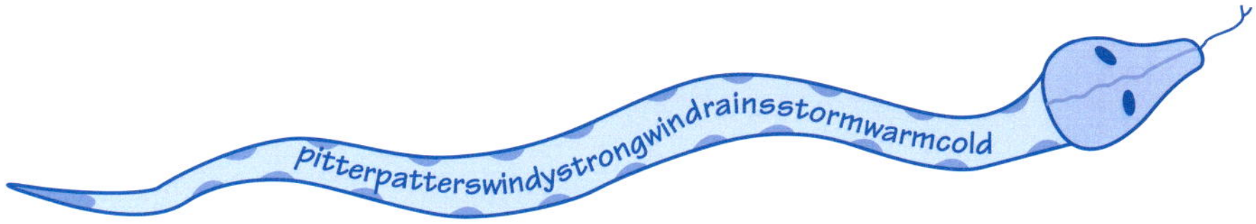

When it's ______________________________, you can fly a kite.

In the summer it's usually ______________________________.

You don't lie on the beach when it's ______________________________.

People often wear wellies when it ______________________________.

You can't go surfing in a ______________________________ because the ______________________________ is too ______________________________.

The rain ______________________________ on the window.

Leben und Sterben

7 Buchstabendreher! Welche Verben verstecken sich hier? Übersetze sie.

edi ____________________ ____________________

eisurvv ____________________ ____________________

nuri ____________________ ____________________

shrac ____________________ ____________________

kins ____________________ ____________________

To bring und *to take*

8 *Bring* oder *take?* Entscheide dich für die richtige Variante.

Can you ______________ me my wellies, please?

I always ________________ my swimsuit on holiday.

________________ the ice-cream here, please.

Can you ________________ him this souvenir?

Wichtige Ausdrücke

9 Welche kleinen Wörter fehlen in diesen Sätzen?

We've got a pier ___________ mile long.

There are lots of shops and cafés in the town ___________ Penzance.

Jack is surfing ___________ the Internet.

We often sing songs ___________ the way home.

Zahlen über 100

Du schreibst:	Du sprichst:
123	a/one hundred and twenty-three
1,010	a/one thousand and ten
33,672	thirty-three thousand six hundred and seventy-two
521,204	five hundred and twenty-one thousand two hundred and four
1,000,000	a/one million

Aufgepasst: Im Englischen steht bei den Tausenderschritten ein Komma, im Deutschen ein Punkt!

Zahlen ausschreiben 38

10 Höre dir die CD an und schreibe die gehörten Zahlen als Ziffern aus.

1. ______________ 3. ______________ 5. ______________

2. ______________ 4. ______________ 6. ______________

Jahreszahlen

Du schreibst:	Du sprichst:
1267	twelve sixty-seven *oder* twelve hundred and sixty-seven
1900	nineteen hundred
2005	two thousand and five

Achtung: *two thousand* kann nicht weggelassen werden!

11 Schreibe die Jahreszahlen, wie man sie spricht. Lass das Wort *hundred* weg, wo es nicht notwendig ist.

1066 ______________________ 1998 ______________________

1324 ______________________ 2000 ______________________

1800 ______________________ 2008 ______________________

Die Gegenwart: Verlaufsform und einfache Form

Das ***simple present*** verwendet man bei:	
gewohnheitsmäßigen Handlungen. Signalwörter: *often, usually, never* usw.:	Sarah often **goes** swimming. I **like** chocolate.
aufeinanderfolgenden Handlungen. Signalwörter: *first, next, after that* usw.:	First Alan **gets up** and then he **goes** downstairs. After that he and his sister **go** to school.
Das ***present progressive*** verwendet man bei:	
gerade ablaufende Handlungen. Signalwörter: *now, look, just, this morning* usw.	I'**m walking** to the beach now. Look! He'**s surfing**. We'**re having** a picnic today.

Zuhören und schreiben 39

12 Höre dir die CD an. Welche Handlungen laufen gerade ab, welche sind gewohnheitsmäßig? Trage die Nummer des Satzes ein.

gewohnheitsmäßig: ______________________

gerade ablaufend: ______________________

Simple present oder *present progressive?*

13 Ein Telefongespräch. Ergänze die richtige Form der Verben.

Martin: Hi Graham. What (you/to do) ______________ now?

Graham: I (to go) ______________ to Cornwall on the train.

Martin: Oh, yes. You (always/to go) ______________ to Cornwall on holiday.

Graham: Yes, I know and we (always/to have) ______________ a good time but we (usually/to go) ______________ by car. It's terrible on the train.

Martin: Why? I (to like) ______________________ trains.

Graham: Yes, but you (not/to go) ______________________ with two little sisters. Listen! They (to sing) ______________________! And they (always/to sing) ______________________ in the car.

14 Jane fährt in die Ferien. Ergänze die richtige Form der Verben.

Jane (to get up) ____________ at 8 o'clock and then (to go) ____________ downstairs. Usually Jane (not/to get up) ________________ early on Saturday but today she (to go) __________ on holiday and she's excited. Her parents (to have) ________________ breakfast in the kitchen now but her brother and sister (still/to sleep) ____________________. Jane (to eat) ____________ her breakfast, (to wash) ____________ her face and then (to pack) ____________ her bag. She's ready. She's so happy because this year she (not/to go) ________________ on holiday with her family, she (to go) ______________ with her friend, Ann and Ann's family. Just then the phone (to ring) ____________ and her mum (to answer) ____________ it. "I'm sorry, Jane, Ann's car (not/to work) ____________ ____________ this morning, so you can't go on holiday with them now. But don't worry, you can come with us."

Jane is not happy. And why is her mum so happy? She (to look) __________ at her mum and her mum suddenly laughs, "No, it was just a joke. They (to come) ____________________ here now so you can get your bags."

Some, any **und** ***no***

In **bejahten Aussagen** verwendet man ***some:***

I've got some postcards.	I habe ein paar Postkarten.
Let's eat some chocolate.	Lass uns etwas Schokolade essen.

In **Fragen** verwendet man ***any:***

Do we need any eggs?	Brauchen wir Eier?
Have you got any wellies?	Habt ihr Gummistiefel?

In verneinten Aussagen kann man ***any*** oder ***no*** (ohne *not!*) verwenden:

He hasn't got any teeth. →
He's got no teeth. → Er hat keine Zähne.

Du kannst das Substantiv auch weglassen, wenn es schon genannt ist: Have you got any postcards? – Yes, we've got some over there.

15 Im Urlaub. Trage *some* oder *any* in die Lücken ein.

Excuse me. Have you got __________ postcards, please?

Yes, we've got __________ over there.

Have you got __________ wellies?

Yes, I've got __________ but I don't know where they are.

Are there __________ rocks in the sea here?

No, there aren't __________ here but there are __________ over there on that beach.

I'd like __________ chocolate now.

Well, you can't have __________.

16 Schreibe die Sätze mit *no* um, wo es möglich ist.

1. I'm sorry. We haven't got any swimsuits.

   ____

2. Are there any restaurants near the beach?

   ____

3. There aren't any lighthouses near here.

   ____

4. I don't know any famous people.

   ____

17 Übersetze den Dialog und verwende *some* oder *any*.

1. Kannst du am Strand Leute sehen?

   ____

2. Nein. Dort sind keine Leute.

   ____

3. Aber ich kann ein paar Menschen auf dem Pier sehen.

   ____

4. Und gibt es Spielautomaten auf den Pier?

   ____

5. Ja, ich glaube, es gibt dort welche.

   ____

Unregelmäßige Pluralformen

Wenn ein Nomen auf *-f* endet, bildest du die Pluralendung meist mit *-ves:*

a thie**f** [f] → two thie**ves** [vz] a scar**f** [f] → four scar**ves** [vz]

Wenn ein Nomen mit einem Konsonant + *y* endet, bildest du die Pluralendung mit *-ies*. Wenn ein Vokal vor dem *y* steht, bleibt es erhalten:

a famil**y** → two famil**ies** a d**ay** → seven d**ays**

Einzeln musst du lernen:

one m**a**n	→	three m**e**n	a child	→	three child**ren**
a wom**a**n	→	four wom**e**n	a fish	→	two **fish**
a f**oo**t	→	two f**ee**t	a person	→	many **people**
a t**oo**th	→	28 t**ee**th			

Wenn du bei diesen Formen den s-Genitiv verwenden willst, hängst du einfach ein **'s** an (statt *s'*):

The men**'s** dogs are playing with a ball. (*Aber:* The boys' sandwiches are tasty.)

18 Wie lautet die Mehrzahl dieser Wörter?

day	________________	diary	________________
hobby	________________	fish	________________
foot	________________	child	________________
tooth	________________	scarf	________________

Singular oder Plural? 40

19 Höre dir die CD an und schreibe die zwölf genannten Wörter auf.

______________________ ______________________

______________________ ______________________

______________________ ______________________

______________________ ______________________

______________________ ______________________

______________________ ______________________

20 Setze diese Sätze in die Mehrzahl. Vorsicht: Auch Verben und Possessivpronomen können sich dabei ändern!

The thief's bag is in his car.

____

The child's bike is red.

____

The baby's bed is small.

____

The woman's shoes look old.

____

I don't know that person's name.

____

Das Wesentliche verstehen

21 Lies den Text über Patricks Urlaub in Cornwall. Was ist die richtige Reihenfolge? Dann beantworte die Fragen mit „richtig“ oder „falsch“.

A
“I can go surfing for a short time,” I think.
I take out the surfboard and it’s great. The waves are excellent and I forget the time. Then suddenly I see that the beach is a long way away so I start swimming towards the beach. I’m tired and I’m scared now. What can I do? There are no people on the beach now and the waves are really big.

B
I usually go surfing with Pete but he can’t go today because he must help his dad. My mum and dad don’t want to go to the beach today, they want to go shopping.
“Can I go to the beach?” I ask Mum. “Yes, OK, but don’t go surfing. A storm is coming from the Atlantic Ocean.” I go to the beach. There aren’t many people there because it’s cold and windy. A few people are walking their dogs and one man is swimming. It’s windy but there’s no storm.

C
Every year we go on holiday to Cornwall. We always stay in a small village near the sea and I like it because I’ve got some friends there now. I love the sea and we always go swimming and surfing. It’s often windy in Cornwall and the waves are usually good. Sometimes we fly a kite and have picnics on the beach, too.

D
I don’t know that my parents are looking for me. They are scared for me because I’m not on the beach and my surfboard isn’t there. They call for help. Suddenly I see a boat. It’s coming towards me. I’m so tired, I can’t climb in the boat. My parents pull *(ziehen)* me in and take me to the beach. I survive but my surfboard breaks on the rocks.

Richtige Reihenfolge der Textabschnitte: ______________________

1. Patrick geht surfen, weil der Sturm noch nicht losgegangen ist. ______________________

2. Patrick wird gerettet, weil seine Eltern merken, dass er surfen gegangen ist. ______________________

Lesen und Informationen heraussuchen

22 Lies dir durch, was im Internet über die Isle of Wight steht, dann beantworte die Fragen.

Come to the Isle of Wight, a beautiful island in the south of England!

We have beautiful sandy beaches all around the island and you can find everything here for a great holiday.

The Isle of Wight is a small island and you can walk around the island or ride your bike all along the coast. We haven't got any mountains here but we've got a beautiful coast, small rivers and harbours.

You can get to the island by boat and boats go every 20 minutes to Ryde in the summer. Ryde is a small town with lots of shops and a pier a mile long. The beach is perfect for children and you can row boats here, build sand castles or catch fish in the sea.

Surfers usually go to the west of the island. The wind is often strong here and the waves high and you can go surfing or windsurfing. Then you can visit St. Catherine's lighthouse and see the Needles. The Needles are big rocks in the sea and tourists often visit them.

Are you interested in castles? Well, come and visit Carisbrooke Castle in the centre of the island or Osborne House near Cowes.

1. Where is the Isle of Wight? ______________________________

2. Are there mountains on the Isle of Wight? ______________________________

3. How can you get to the island? ______________________________

4. What can you do in Ryde? ______________________________

____

5. Where do surfers usually go? And why? ______________________________

____

Zuordnen und zuhören 41

23 In welchen Wörtern kommt der Laut [ɜː] vor? Unterstreiche diese Wörter. Dann höre dir die CD an und überprüfe deine Antwort.

girl	summer	adventure	hear	person
Germany	surf	storm	survive	word
warm	harbour	worry	verb	very

Hören und Informationen heraussuchen 42

24 Kate möchte ein Geschenk kaufen. Höre dir den Dialog an und beantworte dann die Fragen.

1. Who does Kate want to buy a present for?

___

2. What does she think about the bags?

___

3. How much are the bags?

___

4. What does her cousin like?

___

5. How much is the mouse?

___

Hören und schreiben 43

25 Höre dir die folgenden Sätze an und ergänze die Lücken.

Our town is __________ the north of England and it's __________ years old.

Lots of tourists come here every _______________ because it's a great place

for _______________. There are ____________ beautiful beaches near here

and they are good for _______________ because there aren't ______________

in the sea. Many ____________________, old and young, love the interesting

museums in our town. But remember! _______________ your ____________

_________ with you in _______________ because it can be very __________.

Hören und verstehen 44

26 Lies dir die Beschreibungen von Urlaubsorten durch, dann höre dir die CD an. Wo wollen Christine und Mark hinfahren? Wie entscheiden sie sich?

Brighton is a big town on the south coast of England. It's got a long beach, a pier and lots of great shops and cafés. Brighton is a great place for young people and it's only about an hour from London on the train.

Conway is a small town on the north coast of Wales. Lots of tourists come here every year for the beaches and for the mountains. The beaches are safe for children and the mountains aren't too difficult to climb. There are also lots of castles in the north of Wales – fun for all the family.

Do you like rivers and mountains? Do you like old castles and quiet places? Then come to **Llangollen** in North Wales. It's a big village on a river and we've got everything you need for a great holiday. You can walk in the mountains, ride mountain bikes, row boats on the river and visit old castles. Come to Llangollen and make some new friends.

Mark möchte nach _________________, Christine nach _________________.

Sie entscheiden sich für _________________.

Unit 7

Tiere

1 Welche Tiere sind hier abgebildet?

1. 
____

2. 
____

3. 
____

4. 
____

5. 
____

6. 
____

2 Baue aus den Wortteilen ganze Wörter zusammen und schreibe sie in die richtige Lücke.

fa	fie	gra	hor	she	wi	z
ep	ld	ld	ss	rm	oo	se

You can find cows and pigs on a ___________________.

Foxes and birds are ___________________ animals.

You can see monkeys and tigers in a ___________________.

You can ride a ___________________.

Cows and horses usually eat ___________________ in a ___________________.

___________________ usually live outside.

Auf dem Bauernhof

3 Finde die Verben in der Wortschlange! Manche bestehen aus zwei Wörtern. Ergänze die Sätze.

We ______________________ the cows every morning.

I want to ______________________ the horses.

Pigs ______________________ and they love it.

I always ______________________ the baby animals when their mums don't want them.

Sometimes the pigs ______________________ the food.

Körperteile

4 Beschrifte die Bilder.

1. 
____

2. 
____

3. 
____

4. 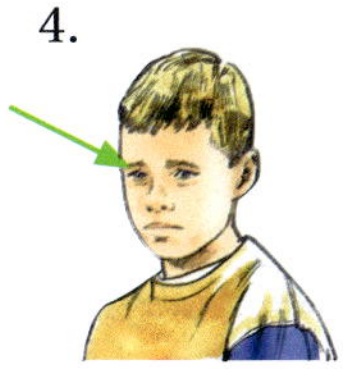
____

5. 
____

6. 
____

Verben

5 Übersetze die Ausdrücke.

ein Foto machen to ____________________

sich (etwas) ausdenken ____________________

hinterherrennen ____________________

erklären ____________________

reparieren ____________________

lächeln ____________________

recht haben ____________________

stehen ____________________

trinken ____________________

Adjektive

6 Finde sieben Adjektive in dem Wortgitter und schreibe sie neben die entsprechende Übersetzung.

besorgt ____________________

traurig ____________________

leer ____________________

tot ____________________

klar ____________________

dunkel ____________________

nervös ____________________

w	f	n	d	z	u	s
c	l	e	a	r	m	a
w	o	r	r	i	e	d
d	y	v	k	j	m	t
e	n	o	d	g	p	e
a	i	u	r	c	t	p
d	l	s	x	n	y	r

Das modale Hilfsverb *must*

Wie bei *can* bleibt *must* bei allen Personen gleich. Fragen bildest du, indem du *must* vor das Subjekt stellst.

I **must** do my homework.	Ich muss meine Hausaufgaben machen.
You **must** go home now.	Du musst jetzt nach Hause gehen.
She **must** have lunch.	Sie muss zu Mittag essen.
Must he feed the pigs?	Muss er die Schweine füttern?

7 Bilde ganze Sätze, indem du die Wörter in die richtige Reihenfolge bringst.

morning – must – do – you – what – in – the – ?

____

feed – must – I – chickens – the

____

my – the – dad – must – milk – cows

____

8 Übersetze diese Sätze.

Musst du den Stall ausmisten?

____

____

Wir müssen uns um die Pferde kümmern.

____

Ihr müsst jetzt die Schafe nach Hause bringen.

____

Mustn't und *needn't*

Die Formen von *mustn't* und *needn't* sind für alle Personen gleich:

You **mustn't** drink that.	Du darfst das nicht trinken.
We **needn't** feed the cows.	Wir brauchen die Kühe nicht zu füttern.

9 Was braucht ein Hund? Ergänze *mustn't* oder *needn't*.

When you buy a dog, you must look after it. You must give it good food and you ________________ give it chocolate every day. It's too sweet. You must walk your dog every day but you ________________ walk for hours. One hour every day is enough. You must wash your dog but you ______________________ wash it in the bathroom – dogs get very dirty! And remember you ________________ get a dog if you are allergic to them.

10 Übersetze diese Sätze.

Hunde dürfen nicht hinter Schafen herrennen.

____

Wir brauchen die Katzen nicht zu füttern.

____

Füchse dürfen keine Hühner fressen.

____

Du brauchst die Pferde nicht zu reiten.

____

Satzstellung

Zeit	Subjekt	Verb	Objekt	Ort	Zeit
On Monday	she	eats	lunch	at school.	
	She	eats	lunch	at school	on Monday.
	We	play	football	in the park	after school.
After school	we	play	football	in the park.	

Normalerweise stehen Orts- und Zeitangaben am Ende des Satzes und **immer** mit **Ort vor Zeit.** Wenn du eine Zeitangabe betonen willst, kannst du sie auch an den Satzanfang stellen.

11 Leben auf dem Bauernhof. Baue Sätze aus den angegebenen Wörtern.

in – in – the – the – the – morning – dad – my – cow shed – cows – milks

____

after – in – breakfast – chickens – mum – garden – my – feeds – the – the

____

eat – half – twelve – the – we – all – past – kitchen – lunch – in – at

____

fields – in – outside – in – the – the – eat – summer – we – often

____

at – sheep – night – the – home – we – bring

____

fields – horses – children – at – in – the – weekend – ride – the – the

____

Satzverknüpfung mit Konjunktionen

Mit *and* und *but* kannst du Hauptsätze verbinden.

Hauptsatz *(main clause)*		Hauptsatz *(main clause)*
Mum feeds the chickens	**and**	she cooks the dinner.
I like animals	**but**	I don't like dogs.

Mit *because, before, when, where* und *so* kannst du einen Hauptsatz mit einem Nebensatz verbinden.

Hauptsatz *(main clause)*	Nebensatz *(subordinate clause)*	
I like cats	**because**	they're funny.
I feed the dog	**when**	I get up.
He rides his horse	**before**	he has breakfast.
My parents work	**so**	we can't have a dog.

Die Wortstellung (Subjekt – Verb – Objekt) bleibt auch im Nebensatz gleich.

12 Ein Urlaub auf dem Bauernhof. Verbinde die Satzteile, die zusammenpassen.

Let's get up early	before we leave.
Let's have breakfast	but I can't ride them.
We must take wellies	and leave early.
Can you wear wellies	because farms are always dirty.
I like horses	so I can phone Rob.
I must take my mobile	when you ride a horse?

13 Gehen wir in den Zoo? Formuliere die Sätze zu einem einzigen um und verwende *and, but, because, before* oder *when.*

Let's go to the zoo. Let's have lunch there.

____

No, we can't have lunch there – it's too expensive.

____

Well, let's make some sandwiches – then we go to the zoo.

____

I like the zoo – there are always too many people there.

____

It's better – the weather's bad.

____

We can go in the monkey house – it rains.

____

14 Übersetze diese Sätze.

Hunde sind lustig, wenn du mit ihnen spielst.

____

Katzen mögen keine Hunde, weil Hunde Katzen jagen.

____

Katzen essen Katzenfutter und sie trinken Milch.

____

Das Wesentliche verstehen

15 Chris fährt in Urlaub. Lies zuerst den Text, dann ordne den einzelnen Abschnitten eine passende Überschrift zu.

Chris gets a pet – Chris starts to like the farm – Help for the dog – Chris is not happy – They get to the farm

1. ______________________________

We're going on holiday today but I don't want to go. I usually like holidays but we usually go to the seaside and I like the sea and I like piers and arcade games. This year we're staying on a farm. Farms! How boring! My little sister likes farms. She likes all the animals but I don't.

2. ______________________________

We get there at 12.30 and eat lunch in the farm's kitchen with the farmer. It's good. Then we go out and look at the farm. We see sheep and horses and pigs and my sister is very excited. She wants to ride a horse. A dog brings me a ball because she wants to play. I don't want to play with a silly dog.

3. ______________________________

In the evening we meet the farmer's two children, Alice and Mark. Alice is eleven and Mark is thirteen. They're nice and we all listen to some music. The next day Mark shows me the tractors and when the farmer drives a tractor to the fields, we go with him. It's great. The silly dog comes with us, too. I think she likes me. We help the farmer in the fields and at lunchtime we have a picnic. The dog has lunch with us, too, but she isn't very happy.

4. ______________________________

In the evening we're all eating in the kitchen when a farmhand runs in and says there's a problem with the dog. The farmer runs out of the kitchen and me and Mark go, too. We find the dog. She is having puppies *(Welpen)*. Two very small dogs are drinking milk from their mummy, but the dog is not happy. They call the vet and thirty minutes later the vet is there. She looks at the dog and says, "There's a big puppy inside her and it can't come out." The vet helps but the puppy is dead. It is very sad.

5. ______________________________

The next day we visit the dogs and her two puppies. She's happy now and she licks my hand. At the end of the week the puppies are not so small and they are really funny. I like them. I want to take a puppy home but I must wait until the puppies are eight weeks old. Eight weeks later we come back to the farm and take a puppy home with us.

Informationen heraussuchen

16 Elizabeth möchte ein Haustier. Lies den Text und beantworte die Fragen.

Elizabeth: Mum, can I have a dog?
Mum: Yes, of course, but you must look after it.
Elizabeth: Great. Thanks, Mum.
Mum: Do you know how to look after a dog?
Elizabeth: Yes, you must feed it in the morning and at night and ...
Mum: And what do they eat?
Elizabeth: Er. Cats?
Mum: Ha ha. You must buy a book on dogs. And read it.
Elizabeth: Yes, OK. And must I take it to the vet's?
Mum: Yes, before you take it out to the park, but you needn't take it alone. We can go together in the car.
Elizabeth: Thanks, Mum. And can I have a big dog, a sheepdog?
Mum: Well, yes, but do you know that sheepdogs need long walks?
Elizabeth: Well, yes, at the weekends, but he needn't go for a walk every day.
Mum: Of course he does. You must take him every morning and every evening.
Elizabeth: Even when it's cold?
Mum: He must go for a walk even when it rains.
Elizabeth: Er, Mum. Can I have a cat, please?

1. Elizabeths Mutter sagt, dass sie einen Hund bekommt, wenn __________

____

2. Was weiß Elizabeth über Hunde? ______________________________

____

3. Was muss Elizabeth kaufen?

____

4. Muss Elizabeth den Hund zum Tierarzt bringen?

____

5. Muss Elizabeth ihn jeden Tag ausführen?

____

Hören und wiederholen 45

17 Höre dir die Satzmelodie an. Geht die Stimme nach oben oder nach unten? Zeichne Pfeile über die Haupt- und Nebensätze.

I've got a camera but I can't take good photos.

I don't need a camera because I can take photos with my mobile.

I want a video camera so that I can make short films.

Hören und schreiben 46

18 Ein Tierpfleger im Zoo erzählt. Höre zu und trage die fehlende Wörter ein.

I work at the ____________ and ____________ a great job. I ____________ start work until nine o'clock but I ____________ get to the zoo at about eight ____________ then I say hello to the ____________. They are like friends. First I ____________ feed them. I always talk to the animals ____________ I feed them. ____________ like that. They ____________ answer, of course, ____________ sometimes I think that they know what I'm saying.

I always play with the ____________ when I see ____________. Monkeys love games and I ____________ they can ____________, too. Then I often ____________ the elephants. The elephants ____________ a walk and I love riding them. Elephants are funny, ____________, but you ____________ watch out with elephants ____________ they can hurt you. I don't play with all the animals, of ____________. For example, I ____________ go ____________ near a tiger.

Hören und verstehen 47

19 Henry und Elaine wollen beide ein Haustier, aber welches? Höre dir den Dialog an, dann beantworte die Fragen mit *true* oder *false*.

1. Henry likes dogs because you can teach them things. ______________
2. Elaine wants to go for a walk with her cat. ______________
3. Elaine thinks cats are interesting. ______________
4. Elaine says that you must wash a dog every day. ______________
5. Henry likes dead mice and birds. ______________
6. They decide to get a cat. ______________

Hören und zuordnen 48

20 Höre dir die einzelnen Wörter auf der CD an. Wie wird das *a* ausgesprochen? Trage die Wörter in die richtige Spalte ein.

animal – farm – same – activity – grass – bacon – hand – bad – take – famous – half – dark

[æ]	[eɪ]	[ɑː]
______________	______________	______________
______________	______________	______________
______________	______________	______________
______________	______________	______________
______________	______________	______________

Revision C (Unit 6 – 7)

Menschen und Tiere

1 Ordne die folgenden Menschen und Tiere der richtigen Spalte zu.

cat – cow – farmhand – dog – grandad – tourist – half-sister – mouse – parents – pig – visitor – sheep – teacher – vet – woman

family	people with jobs	other people	farm animals	pets
___	___	___	___	___
___	___	___	___	___
___	___	___	___	___

Adjektive

2 Suche zehn Adjektivpaare aus dem Kasten heraus und übersetze sie.

bad	boring	calm	short	cheap
terrible	expensive	good	great	happy
large	long	loud	nervous	right
sad	small	wrong	interesting	quiet

___ – ___ ___ – ___

___ – ___ ___ – ___

___ – ___ ___ – ___

___ – ___ ___ – ___

___ – ___ ___ – ___

Verben mit zwei Wörtern

3 Das Leben auf einen Bauernhof. Ergänze die fehlenden Wörter.

I'd like to live ________ a farm and I often think ________ my holidays there. Before I go to the farm, I always take ________ my shoes and try ________ my old wellies. You need wellies on a farm because it's always dirty. When I get ________ the farm, I always go and look ________ Shep, the old dog. He's my friend and he always asks ________ a biscuit. In the morning I always wake ________ early and then I look ________ the chickens. Sometimes I muck ________ the pigs, too, but never before breakfast. The pigs are funny, I think. They always fight ________ their breakfast. When I'm at home, I always talk ________ the farm to my friends. Sometimes I want to run ________ and go to the farm again but I know that I must go to school. But when I'm 16 …

Zeitangaben

4 Du kennst nun schon viele Wörter und Ausdrücke, um zu sagen, wann oder wie oft etwas passiert. Übersetze!

schon	________	sofort	________
erste/r/s	________	alle (zehn Tage)	*e*________ (ten days)
nächste/r/s	________	immer	________
später	________	nie	________
im Augenblick	________	manchmal	________
bevor	________	oft	________

Zeit und Ort

5 Welche Präposition ist richtig? Ergänze die Sätze mit *on, in, at, from* oder *to.*

I often play tennis __________ the weekend.

School finishes __________ half past three.

I always get up late __________ Saturday.

What do you usually do __________ the evening?

What's __________ TV now?

I like to sit __________ the beach __________ summer.

I usually walk __________ home __________ school.

Nützliche Ausdrücke

6 Verbinde die Sätze miteinander, so dass sich sinnvolle Kombinationen ergeben.

How are you?	It's five thirty.
I like Jim.	What a mess!
What time is it, please?	He's fed up.
That's one pound fifty, please.	London.
Look at your room!	He's a pain.
John's not happy.	He's great fun.
I don't like my brother.	I'm fine, thanks.
Where are you from?	Here you are.

7 Janet und ihre Familie. Ergänze die Lücken mit den richtigen Formen von *to be, have got* und den passenden Personalpronomen.

Rob: Have you ___________ any sisters, Janet?

Janet: No, I _______________ but ___________ got a brother. His name ___________ Tony.

Rob: Oh, how old ___________ he?

Janet: ___________ twenty-two. And ___________ got two children.

Rob: So ___________ an aunt and ___________ only twelve! How old ___________ his children?

Janet: ___________ one and three. They ___________ (not) very interesting.

Die Gegenwart: Verlaufsform und einfache Form

8 Übersetze den Dialog.

Schau mal! Was machen die Vögel dort?

____

Sie warten auf etwas zu essen.

____

Samstags kommen sie immer hierher.

____

Warum kommen sie samstags hierher?

____

Weil meine Mutter am Wochenende nicht kocht.

____

Word order

9 Im Urlaub. Bilde Sätze, indem du die Wörter in die richtige Reihenfolge bringst.

1. always – because – early – I – go – needn't – get – school – up – I – to

____

2. breakfast – the – we – warm – when – often – have – it's – in – garden

____

3. usually – go – in – to – summer – Scotland – we

____

4. my – cold – brother – never – because – swims –it's – the – in – too – sea

____

5. 11 o'clock – dark – doesn't – it – in – get – Scotland – until

____

Hilfsverben

10 Das Leben eines Hundes. *Can, can't, must, mustn't* oder *needn't?* Ergänze.

A dog's life is great. I __________ get up late and I __________ go to school. I __________ sleep when I want and eat when I'm hungry. I __________ look after the house and I __________ break things but I __________ sleep on the sofa. And at the weekend I __________ watch Chris play tennis in the park, but I __________ play, of course. And I __________ chase the ball, says Chris.

Mengenangaben

11 *Much/many, some/any/no, a few/a little* – Unterstreiche das richtige Wort.

Nina: We've got a few/a little cheese sandwiches but have we got any/ some crisps?

David: Yes, we've got any/some crisps but we haven't got any/some apples.

Nina: OK. Here you are. Oh, and we haven't got much/many chocolate.

David: No, we must buy any/some. And we've only got a few/a little water.

Nina: There's any/some here. But we've got any/no tins of cola.

David: Well, we don't need many/much tins. I don't like it. Is that everything?

Nina: Oh no. What about our clothes?

Der Genitiv

12 *Of*-Genitiv oder *s*-Genitiv? Übersetze.

Das Haus meines Onkels ist da drüben.

____

Das Name des Hauses ist Seaview.

____

Die Fahrräder meiner Cousinen sind im Garten.

____

Am ersten Tag der Ferien gehen sie immer zum Strand.

____

Zuhören und schreiben 49

13 Ann möchte ein Zimmer in einem Hotel reservieren. Höre dir das Telefongespräch an, dann fülle das Formular und Anns Notizzettel aus.

Hotel Seaview

Name of visitor:

____

Phone number:

____

Dates:
From ______________ to

____

Hotel Seaview

Price of room: ______________ *a night or* ______________ *a week*

Number of rooms: ________

At hotel: ______________________

Address: ______________________

Hotel closes at ______________________

Übersetzen

14 Lili schickt ihrer englischen Freundin eine E-Mail. Übersetze.

Hallo Jenny,

möchtest du mich im August besuchen? Im Sommer regnet es nicht oft, daher können wir jeden Tag im Meer schwimmen gehen. Normalerweise nehmen wir im Sommer ein Picknick *(Plural!)* mit an den Strand, und am Wochenende segeln wir oft mit *(in)* dem Boot meines Vaters. Komm doch bitte! Im August ist es hier richtig toll *(fun)*.

Lili

____

____

____

Schreiben

15 Auf dem Bauernhof. Schau dir die Bilder genau an und beschreibe, was du siehst. Achtung: Welche Zeitform musst du jeweils verwenden?

Usually ______________________ Today ______________________

______________________ ______________________

______________________ ______________________

______________________ ______________________

______________________ ______________________

______________________ ______________________

Zuhören und verstehen 50

16 Kylie ruft Ben an. Höre dir das Gespräch an und beantworte die Fragen mit *true* oder *false*.

1. Ben goes surfing every morning. ______________________
2. Ben is having a picnic on the beach. ______________________
3. It's raining in England now. ______________________
4. Ben is on holiday in England. ______________________
5. Kylie gets a shock because she's calling him on her mobile. ______________________

Unit 1

1 1 – one; 6 – six; 9 – nine; 12 – twelve; 18 – eighteen; 21 – twenty-one; 28 – twenty-eight; 30 – thirty; 36 – thirty-six; 44 – forty-four; 55 – fifty-five; 80 – eighty; 83 – eighty-three; 100 – one hundred

2 Hello. **My** name is Ann. – Hello.
What's **your** name? – John.
How **old** are you? – I'm twelve.
Where are you from? – I'm from Paris.
What's your phone number? – It's 863 2119.

3 boy, teacher, mum, girl
caretaker, tutor, friend, pupil

4

r	**l**	**i**	**s**	**t**	**e**	**n**
e	**p**	**l**	**a**	**y**	p	**f**
a	r	h	w	o	k	**i**
d	r	a	t	e	**p**	**n**
w	**r**	**i**	**t**	**e**	**h**	**d**
q	a	**c**	a	g	**o**	b
s	**h**	**o**	**u**	**t**	**n**	v
a	u	**p**	y	f	**e**	m
y	i	**y**	**m**	**a**	**k**	**e**

abschreiben – to copy; finden – to find; sagen – to say; schreiben – to write; lesen – to read; zuhören – to listen; machen – to make; schreien – to shout; anrufen – to phone; spielen – to play

5 apple; pencil; ruler; exercise book; rubber; pencil case; pen

6 1. cafeteria; 2. playground; 3. ball; 4. lunchtime; 5. classroom; 6. lesson; 7. tutor group; 8. pupil; 9. primary school; 10. teacher; 11. caretaker; 12. schoolbag

7 window; wall; poster; board; desk; door; cupboard; table; chair

8 The apple is **on** the table.
The pencils are **under** the table.
There are some books **in** the cupboard.
There is a poster **on** the wall.
The chair is **behind** the desk.

9 Sorry I'm late.
Sit down, please.
You're welcome.
What's for homework, please?
Can I go to the toilet, please?
Where are we?

10 höflich – polite; anders – different; langweilig – boring; beängstigend – scary; richtig – right; groß – big; glücklich – lucky; leicht – easy
English is not **terrible.**

11 I – ich; you – du, Sie, ihr; he – er; she – sie; it – es; they – sie; we – wir

12 I **am** eleven.
This is Emma. She **is** my friend.
We **are** from London.
Hello John. You **are** in my tutor group.
John **is** from Bristol.
My new school **is** big.
That is Francisco and this is Maria. They **are** from Spain.

13 They are nice.
She is new here.
Tom is my friend.
I am eleven.
This is Lisa.

14
1. She is my teacher.
2. Henry and William are nice.
3. I am in your class.
4. Football is my favourite sport.

15 1. They're in the classroom.
2. It's a football.
3. I'm from Madrid.
4. You're in the wrong room.
5. We're eleven.

16 **I'm** in Year 5.
He is nice.
She's in my tutor group, too.
They're in my bag.
We are late.

17 1. I am not eleven.
2. It is not a football.
3. They are not late.
4. You are not my friend.
5. She is not from Greenwich.

18 Maria **isn't** ten. **She's** eleven.
Rob**'s** from London. He **isn't** from Cardiff.
They **aren't** pupils. **They're** teachers.
That's a book. It **isn't** a poster.

19 Are we late?
Is he your friend?
Are they your shoes?

20 Am I lucky? – Yes, you are.
Is he from Greenwich? – No, he isn't.
Are they new here, too? – Yes, they are.
Are you always late? – No, I'm not.

21 **Are** you a teacher? – No, **I'm not.**
Is that your pen? – Yes, **it is.**
Are they in your bag? – No, **they aren't.**

22 Is that **an** English book? – No, it's **a** German book.
Here's **a** sandwich and here's **an** apple.
That isn't **a** pen. It's **an** old pencil. It's **a** useful thing.

23 1. [ði:]; 2. [ðə]; 3. [ðə]; 4. [ðə]; 5. [ðə]; 6. [ði:]; 7. [ðə]; 8. [ði:]

24 [s] : groups, crisps, units
[z] : schools, folders, phones
[ɪz] : pencil-cases, boxes, buses

25 [s] : desks, books, lists
[z] : games, numbers, friends
[ɪz] : exercises, sandwiches, pages

26 **There are** twenty classrooms in the school. **There are** twelve tables in one classroom. **There is/There's** a bag on one table. **There is/There's** a book in the bag. **There are** fifty-five pages in the book. On one page **there is/there's** a picture. In the picture **there is/there's** a school.

27 There is one apple.
There are three pens.
There are five pencils.
There is one ruler.
There are two rubbers.
There is one pencil-case.

28 **What** is that? – It's a mouse.
Where are you **from?** – I'm from Greenwich.
Who is that? – It's Lisa.
How old are you? – I'm eleven.
Where is the teacher? – She's in the classroom.
What is on the desk? – There are two books.

29
1. Where is your apple?
2. What's on the table?
3. Who is in the classroom?
4. How old is Tom?
5. Where is the teacher from?
6. Who is Mr Cash?

30 1. richtig; 2. falsch; 3. falsch; 4. falsch; 5. richtig; 6. richtig

31

	five	5		fifteen	15		forty-four	44
+	seven	7	+	ten	10	+	thirty-three	33
+	eight	8	+	thirteen	13	+	two	2
=	twenty	20	=	thirty-eight	38	=	seventy-nine	79

32 Beschreibung C stimmt mit dem Bild überein.

33

Nicola: Look. There's Paul.
Fiona: Is he **new** here?
Nicola: Yes, he is. He's from Manchester. He's **cool.**
David: Cool? No, he isn't. His jokes are **boring.**
Nicola: No, they aren't. And he's nice.
Fiona: Is he in Year 7, **too?**
Nicola: Yes, he is, but he **isn't** in my tutor group.
Fiona: And what's his **favourite** sport?
Nicola: It's football. And this is his **ball.**
David: Oh, good. Let's **play** now.
Nicola: But David. Paul isn't your **friend.**
David: Oh. **He's** OK.

34

Hi. I'm Jackie and I'm **eleven.** Ann is my friend and she's **twelve.** I'm at Greenwich School and it's very big. There are **forty** classrooms in my school. There are **twenty-eight** pupils in my class and we're lucky – there are **twenty-nine** chairs. Mr Ellis is my teacher. He's **fifty-three.**

35

6 Yes, he is. He's cool.
3 Yes, I am. I'm in Mr Carter's tutor group.
1 Hi. I'm Emma. What's your name?
2 My name's Jimmy. Are you in Year 7, too?
5 I'm from Madrid. Is Mr Carter nice?
4 Oh, good. Mr Carter's my tutor, too. Where are you from?

36

1. richtig; 2. falsch; 3. richtig; 4. falsch; 5. falsch

Unit 2

1 Look at Tracy Spencer's family **tree.** She has got a big family. Sarah Spencer is her **grandma.** Tim Spencer and Rachel Smith are her **parents.** They have got three **children.** Tracy's **uncle** is David Spencer and he is **divorced** from her **aunt,** Elena Stavros. She has got one **cousin,** Samuel, and he is an **only** child. Tracy isn't an only child. She has got one **brother,** Phil and one **sister,** Susan.

2 1. upstairs, downstairs, window, door, garden
2. shed
3. flat, shop

3 bed, sofa, drums, table, wardrobe, computer, television

4

R	W	**E**	**N**	**G**	**L**	**A**	**N**	**D**
U	G	**G**	**R**	**E**	**E**	**C**	**E**	G
S	A	**T**	**U**	**R**	**K**	**E**	**Y**	R
S	Y	K	C	**M**	J	H	Z	E
I	P	**F**	**R**	**A**	**N**	**C**	**E**	E
A	L	B	T	**N**	E	L	D	K
I	**T**	**A**	**L**	**Y**	I	A	X	N

Russia, England, Greece, Turkey, Italy, Germany, France

5 England – English; Germany – German; Greece – Greek; Italy – Italian; France – French; Russia – Russian; Turkey – Turkish

6 1. listen; 2. sort; 3. open; 4. match; 5. help; 6. underline; 7. play

7 I'm interested in music.
My brother is a pain.
She's in a hurry.
What a mess.

How can I do my homework?
Let's take turns.
Let's have a party.
My sister is good with dogs.
She is fed up.

8 klein – small; schön – beautiful; langsam – slow; beschäftigt – busy; schmutzig – dirty; großartig – great; glücklich – lucky; albern – silly; leise – quiet

9 Let's look at a **photo.**
Let's read a **magazine.**
I've got an **idea.**
Let's play in a **group.**
I can finish my **project.**
Let's listen to **music.**

10 Helen**'s** book is great.
The pupil**s'** names are John and Jill.
The girl**'s** T-shirts are in her wardrobe.
The Elliot**s'** flat is over a shop.
Tom**'s** drums are in his bedroom.

11 The boys' homework is easy.
The cat's name is Tiger.
Helen's CDs are on the table.
The girl's photos are in her bag.

12 I'm Susan and this is **my** sister. **Her** name is Ann.
Is that **your** dog, Ben? – Yes, it is, and that's **its** ball.
Phil and Chris, what's **your** dad's name? – **His** name is Theo.
There are my cousins. They're in **their** garden.

13 **You're** silly and **your** jokes are funny.
They're my friends and **their** house is next to my house.
That's our house. **It's** small but its garden is big.
He's new here and **his** sister is in my tutor group.

14 My name is Kevin. I **have got** one sister and one brother. We **have got** a house in Greenwich. It is small but it **has got** a big garden. My sister **has got** her own room but my brother and I are in one room. That's a problem. My parents **have got** a computer shop and so we **have got** five computers in our house. I **have got** three mice, my sister **has got** a cat and my brother **has got** a dog. They are not friends.

15 **You have got** a green house.
He's got a nice step-father.
They have got three televisions.
She has got a new CD.
I've got a big problem.

16 I**'ve got** a bed but I **haven't got** a sofa in my room.
She**'s got** a table but she **hasn't got** a computer in her room.
They **haven't got** a bike but they**'ve got** a football in their shed.
He**'s got** a wardrobe but he **hasn't got** drums in his room.

17 I **have got** a pen but I **haven't got** a pencil.
She **hasn't got** new shoes but she **has got** a new T-shirt.

18 Have you got a TV in your room?
Susan has not got two sisters.
Has your house got big windows?
I have got two new CDs.

19 Have you got two grandads? – Yes, **I have/we have**.
Have your cousins got a big house? – No, **they haven't**.
Has Lizzie got new shoes? – Yes, **she has**.
Has your garden got a shed in it? – No, **it hasn't**.

20 Don't open the wardrobe.
Watch out in here.
Don't use our computer.
Do our homework, please.
Don't read our exercise books.

21 1. Take turns.
2. Be quiet, please.
3. Don't play football here.

22 She **can't play football** but she **can play the drums**.
They **can write on the board** but they **can't write on the wall**.
The cat **can't talk** but it **can listen.**

23 Can I use your mobile, please? – No, **you can't**.
Can Emma write a sentence in Turkish? – Yes, **she can**.
Can we have a party? – No, **you can't**.

24 Can I listen to your new CD? – Yes, you can.
Can we play in the shed? – No, we can't.
Can you put my mobile in your bag? – Yes, I can.
Can your grandad use a computer? – Yes, he can.
Can you say a sentence in French? – No, I can't, but I can say a sentence in Russian.

25 I **can't** do my homework.
You **can't** draw in my book.
She **can** listen to music in her room.
Tom **can't** play this game.
We **can** have a party.
Jackie **can** help you.

26 1. falsch, 2. richtig; 3. falsch; 4. falsch, 5. richtig, 6. falsch

27 Bill is Melanie's **uncle**. – Christine is Melanie's **grandma**. – John is Melanie's **dad**.

28 *Reihenfolge:* My family – My house – My room – Rules

29 1. ja; 2. nein; 3. ja

30 *keine Lösung*

31 Mike, **can** I **go** in your room, please?
Yes, you **can,** but **don't** use my computer.

I'm not **happy.** I **can't** find my bag.
Oh, I can **help** you.
Thanks. Let's **look** in my room.
Oh no. What a **mess!**

Ann, have you **got** my new T-shirt?
No, I haven't, but **you've** got my discman.
No, I **haven't**. **Dad's** got it.
Dad?

Hey! **Don't** play with my drums.
Oh, please. **Can** I play with **them**?
Oh OK.

32 Bild 1 – Dialog 3; Bild 2 – Dialog 1; Bild 3 – Dialog 2; Bild 4 – Dialog 4

33 1. falsch; 2. richtig; 3. falsch; 4. richtig; 5. richtig; 6. falsch

Unit 3

1

c	**o**	**o**	**k**	**i**	**n**	**g**	n	**b**
l	a	**f**	w	t	u	i	p	**i**
u	**c**	**i**	**n**	**e**	**m**	**a**	q	**k**
b	d	**l**	s	a	j	s	w	**e**
u	b	**m**	s	e	h	x	b	m
m	**s**	**w**	**i**	**m**	**m**	**i**	**n**	**g**
l	u	e	n	j	w	p	t	z
p	e	y	**g**	**u**	**i**	**t**	**a**	**r**
d	**a**	**n**	**c**	**e**	a	v	c	g

cooking; cinema; club; film; swimming; guitar; dance; bike

2 watch a film; play a game; read a book; go to the cinema; ride a bike; sing a song; play the guitar; go swimming

3 7.30: I wake up. – 7.35: I get up. – 7.40: I wash my face. – 7.45: I have breakfast. – 8.15: I go to school. – 12.30: I eat my lunch. – 15.30: I go home. – 20.30: I go to bed. – 20.45: I go to sleep.

4 On Fridays I get up and then I **feed** my dog. He always has breakfast first! Then I **walk** to school. I usually **eat** sandwiches at school for lunch. After school I always **walk the dog** first and then I sometimes **visit** friends. In the evening I often **watch** TV and then I **go to bed** late because we have no school in the morning.

5 **What time is it, please**? – It's half past nine.
What time is the computer club? – It's **from** three thirty **to** half past four.
What day is cooking club? – It's **on Tuesdays**.
When can we meet? – How about **at the weekend**?
We start school at 9 o'clock and we always go home **at half past three**.
I often fall asleep at 9 **pm**.

6 always ⟶ usually ⟶ often ⟶ sometimes ⟶ never

7 to remember, to forget, to like, to love, to look

8

w	u	**c**	**a**	**l**	**l**
g	t	**h**	f	**s**	**o**
t	**e**	**a**	**c**	**h**	**o**
s	x	**s**	t	**o**	**k**
a	k	**e**	o	**w**	**i**
b	**r**	**i**	**n**	**g**	**c**
p	m	z	r	n	**k**

Can you **show** me your photos?
We often **kick** a football in the park.
I can **teach** you a trick.
Can you **bring** me my bag, please?
Dogs often **chase** cats.
You **look** nice.
My cat always comes when I **call** her name.

9 OK. We can meet at 10 in the park. – Great. **See you there.**
How are you? – I'm OK, thanks.
Hi. **It's Emma here.** – Oh, hi. Where are you?
Can we watch a film now? – No. **It's time to go home.**
Can you help me? I can't find Molly. – Yes. Oh, look! **There she is.**
Is Paul nice? – Yes. **He's great fun.**

10 Er traut seinen Augen nicht.
Wie wäre es mit Mittagessen?/Sollen wir mittagessen?
… wie wäre es mit Samstag?
Was kommt im Fernsehen?

11 01.15: one fifteen – quarter past one
06.40: six forty – twenty to seven
03.12: three twelve – twelve minutes past three
09.35: nine thirty-five – twenty-five to ten
02.25: two twenty-five – twenty-five past two
08.30: eight thirty – half past eight
11.55: eleven fifty-five – five to twelve
10.48: ten forty-eight – twelve minutes to eleven

12 1. quarter past nine; 2. twelve minutes to eleven; 3. half past three; 4. quarter to eight; 5. twenty-five past five; 6. twenty to two; 7. five to seven; 8. five past four

13
1. 8.05
2. 10.27
3. 13.45
4. 9.55
5. 7.18
6. 3.25
7. 10.50
8. 12.30
9. 12.00

14
1. I get up at 8 o'clock.
2. On Tuesday you never go swimming.
3. We always walk to school.
4. You play the drums at the weekend.
5. They play football in the park.
6. Patrick and Sophie listen to music.

15 Kylie **gets up** at 7.30 and then **washes** her face. She has breakfast and then **feeds** her cat. She **goes** to school at 8 o'clock because school **starts** at 8.30. School **finishes** at 3.15 and Kylie **goes home** again. Sometimes she **does** her homework then and sometimes she **meets** her friends in the park. In the evening she often **plays** games with her brother and sometimes she **watches** TV.

16 She likes dancing.
She never teaches her brother tricks.
She often goes to the cinema.

17 [s]: forgets; gets up; likes; sleeps; walks
[ɪz]: calls; happens; loves; remembers; runs
[ɪz]: chases; finishes; teaches; washes; watches

18 My sister and I are very different. She **likes** cats and I **like** dogs. She **gets up** early and I **get up** late. She **walks** to school but I **run.** She **does** her homework at home on her desk. I **do** my homework at school in the playground. She always **washes** her face but I often **forget.** She **goes** to dancing lessons and I **play** football. But, yes, I am a girl, too.

19 Kitty often goes swimming.
She meets her friends on Saturday.
She helps her dad in his shop.
She plays basketball on Sunday.
She walks her dog in the park.
She never goes to be early.

20 Ben never goes swimming on Saturday.
In the morning he reads a good book in his shed in the garden.
On Sunday he often stays in bed late.
His friends usually come to his house in the afternoon.
He always watches television in the evening.

21 On Thursday Ellen always plays tennis./Ellen always plays tennis on Thursday.
Ellen's brother runs to school every day. Every day Ellen's brother runs to school.
Ellen's parents usually go swimming at the weekend./At the weekend ...
They often play football in the park on Sunday afternoon./On Sunday afternoon they often play ...
They always watch television in the living room on Sunday./On Sunday they always watch ...
They always watch football.

22 **That** is my house over there.
These are Henry's cards here.
This is your bag here.
Those are my pencils over there.

23 1. **These** are my drums here. 2. **That**'s Kim's football. 3. **This** is Pete's dog.
4. **Those** are your books.

24 1. falsch; 2. richtig; 3. falsch; 4. richtig; 5. richtig; 6. falsch; 7. richtig;
8. richtig

25
2 at half past eight.
6 and it's never boring.
8 and, well, that's sometimes fun.
3 Breakfast at nine
1 I get up late
9 I watch TV from eight to ten
4 and we're all fine.
5 I meet friends in the morning
7 After lunch I help my mum
10 and then it's time for bed again.

26 Kate's favourite day is **Saturday**.

27
Fred‿often gets‿up‿at 8‿o'clock.
Fred‿and his friends sometimes play football‿in the park.
He usually reads‿a book‿in the evening.
Fred has got‿a cat‿and‿a dog.
Fred's cat‿often chases the dog.
They‿always sleep‿on his bag.

28
[θ]: thirteen; thanks, Thursday; thirty; bathroom; three
[ð]: this; together; those; brother; there; the

29 Julie talks about **Saturday**.

30 1. richtig; 2. falsch; 3. falsch; 4. richtig; 5. falsch; 6. richtig

Revision A (Unit 1 – 3)

1

1. an apple
2. a pencil
3. an exercise book
4. a photo
5. a magazine
6. a rubber ball
7. a box
8. an orange crystal
9. an old tin
10. a ruler

2

1. 9.15
2. 11.38
3. 2.48
4. 10.30
5. 1.13
6. 5.25
7. 8.40
8. 3.45
9. 6.03
10. 11.59
11. 2.14
12. 12.20

3

family: parents – Eltern; step-mother – Stiefmutter; half-brother – Halbbruder; aunt – Tante; uncle – Onkel; cousin – Cousin/Cousine
school: caretaker – Hausmeister/-in; rubber – Radiergummi; lesson – Unterrichtsstunde; board – Tafel; desk – Schreibtisch; cafeteria – Café

4

new – old; big – small; short – long; early – late; great – terrible; right – wrong; funny – boring

5

to ride a bike
to have a party
to play cards
to listen to a CD
to spell a word

to do your homework
to learn by heart
to take turns

6 He is always in his shed.
Don't play football in your bedroom.
What have you got in that bag?
She has not got her own room.
Can I help you in the kitchen?
We often play cards in the evening.

7 What's your name? – Mr Johnson.
How old are you? – 21.
Can you play the drums? – Yes, I can.
Where are you from? – Bristol.
What's this? – It's your homework.
Have you got a dog? – Yes, I have.
Where is your dog? – It's at home.
Who is that? – That's the caretaker.
Am I late? – Yes, you are.

8 I **get up** at 7.45. I **am** late. School **starts** at 8.30. I **wash** my face and then I **make** breakfast. I **take** my breakfast into the living room and then **go** upstairs. I can't **find** my bag. My dog **eats** my breakfast. I **run** to school. It **is** 8.35. Oh no. I **go** into the classroom and **say**, "OK boys and girls. We can start now."

9 1. richtig; 2. falsch; 3. falsch; 4. falsch; 5. richtig

10
1 Hi Brian. It's Tim here. How are you?
2 Hi Tim. I'm fine. And you?
3 Fine. Can you play football at the weekend?
4 Yes, I can. Why?
5 We've got a game on Saturday afternoon and Alan can't play.
6 Oh, but you know, I'm not good at football.
7 You're OK. And have you got a ball?
8 Yes, I have. I can bring it with me.
9 OK. Great. See you then.
10 See you.

11 1. falsch; 2. richtig; 3. richtig; 4. richtig; 5. falsch; 6. richtig

12 Peter gets up at 7 o'clock and then feeds his dog. After that he has/eats breakfast.
At 10 o'clock Peter walks his dog and at 2 o'clock he plays football with his friends and his dog in the park. In the evening Peter and his dog usually watch television.

Unit 4

1 1. swimming pool; 2. map; 3. information centre; 4. church; 5. Underground; 6. castle; 7. sweet shop; 8. river; 9. market; 10. museum; 11. bridge; 12. police station
Lösungswort: Cutty Sark

2 Excuse me. Where's the church? – It's **next to** the café.
Is the café **near** the castle? – Yes, it is.
How can I get to the church? – **Go down** Castle Road and then **turn left** into Mouse Road and the church is **on the right.**
Where's the sweet shop, please? – It's **opposite** the police station.
Can I **take** the bus to the café? – Yes, you can. There's the bus stop.
How can I get to the sweet shop, please? – **Go down** Castle Road and then **turn right** into Mouse Road. The sweet shop is **on the left.**

3 **Excuse me.** Where's the police station, please? – I'm sorry. I **don't know.**
The castle is in Orinoco Road. It's opposite the café and next to a museum. – Er sorry, but **can you repeat that, please?**
Can I ask you a question? – Yes, of course.
How can I get to the river? – You can walk there or you can take the bus.
When does the bus go? – There are buses **every** twenty **minutes.**

4 north – west – east – south

5 to sail – segeln; to hurry up – sich beeilen; to catch (a train) – (einen Zug) nehmen; to drive – fahren; to park – parken

6 I want to **ask for** some information.
Can you **repeat** that, please?
I **think** the café is near here.
What does GMT **mean?**
What do you **call** that place?
Can you **guess** how many people live here?

7 arbeiten – to work; korrigieren – to correct; aufschreiben – to write down; kämpfen – to fight

8 Buckingham Palace? Oh yes. I want to visit **it.**
Which funny girls? I can't see **them.**
There's a man. Let's ask **him.**
What about Gemma? Let's get **her** a present.
Let's take a taxi. Excuse me. Can you take **us** to the Thames Barrier, please?

9 Hello. **I**'m a taxi driver and I can show **you** everywhere in London. Come with **me** and listen. Do you know Madonna? Well, that's her house. I often see **her** in the garden. Lots of tourists want to see her house and I often bring **them** in my taxi. I don't think **she** likes that. And do you know Robbie Williams? There's his house. Can you see **it** behind the trees? I don't like **him,** but his songs are great. What do you think?

10 I don't like school.
You don't speak Italian.
Harry and Ginny don't drive to school.
We don't go swimming at 7 o'clock.

11 No, you don't play football every weekend.
No, you're not good at football.
No, you cannot/can't play the guitar.
No, you have not/haven't got a lot of friends.
No, you don't do your homework.
No, Pete and Fred don't like you.

12 Do you like Greenwich Park?
Do you live near the park?
Do tourists often visit the Cutty Sark?
Do people walk under the Thames?
Do we take the Underground to Canary Wharf?

13 **Do** you **live** here? – No, I **don't.** I live in west London.
Do you often **come** here? – Yes, I **do.** I come here every week. My parents live near here.
Do they like it here? – Yes, **they do.**
Do you drive here? – No, I **don't.** I take the Underground.

14 Do some boys come here with their skateboards every week? – Yes, they do.
Can you see the Thames from Greenwich Park? – Yes, you can.
Has one museum got a lot of old clocks? – Yes, it has.
Do a lot of tourists come here in summer? – Yes, they do.
Do some people have lunch in the café? – Yes, they do.

15 Glenda doesn't live in Greenwich.
Glenda doesn't watch football on TV.
Glenda doesn't go to museums.
Glenda doesn't read books in the evening.

16 Does she live near Greenwich Park? – Yes, she does.
Does she come from Italy? – Yes, she does.
Does she like English food? – No, she doesn't.
Does she go to the park with her skateboard? – Yes, she does.

17 Hello. Your grandma comes from Italy. **Does** she speak Italian to you?
Yes, she **does,** but she speaks English, too.
Does she like England?
Yes, she **does,** but she **doesn't** like English food.
Does she often go to the park?
Yes, she **does.** She **goes** there with her skateboard.
And **does** she go fast?
No, she **doesn't** and it looks very funny because she always listens to her discman on her skateboard.

18 Have you got a skateboard? – Yes, I have.
Does it go fast? – Yes, it does.
Is there a place for skateboards near you? – No, there isn't.
Can you use it in the park? – Yes, I can.
Do your parents like it? – No, they don't.
Do you take it to school? – No, I don't.

19 Do you go to school by bus?
My mum takes me to school.
Does your dad take the Underground to work?
My dad doesn't go by Underground.
Do you friends walk to school?
No, my friends don't walk to school.

20
1. When does the café open?
2. How do you get (here)?
3. Who do you meet (here)?
4. What do you do/play (here)?
5. Where do you play football?
6. Why does your dog like it here?

21
1. No, it isn't.
2. Because it's beautiful.
3. On a bridge.
4. People swim and jump into the river.
5. Big ships don't go down the river because it's a small river.
6. You can visit a castle, a cathedral, interesting museums and shops.
7. Yes, there is. The cathedral.
8. Part of the cathedral.
9. By train.
10. Two hours.

22 *Reihenfolge:* C – A – E – D – B

23 [w]: week, water, wash, well, white
[v]: visitor, evening, vocabulary, over, living room

24 *von oben nach unten:*
D – J – B – F – C – G – E – I – A – H

25 *von oben nach unten:*
market, flower shop, information centre, swimming pool

26
1. In Church Street.
2. Yes, it is.
3. At 8 o'clock.
4. Because he can't go swimming before school.
5. In the sea.
6. No, he doesn't.

Unit 5

1 1. size; 2. clothes; 3. money; 4. pence; 5. expensive; 6. medium; 7. try; 8. large
Lösungswort: shopping

2 Excuse me. Have you got this T-shirt in medium? – **Yes, here you are.**
How much is this pen, please? – It's two pounds fifty.
Excuse me, do you sell sweatshirts? – Yes, they're over there.
I'd like to try on these sweatshirts, please. – OK, but you can only take three things.

3 January, February, March, April, May, June, July, August, September, October, November, December

4 1. the first of March; 2. the fifth of June; 3. the eighteenth of January; 4. the eleventh of September; 5. the thirteenth of July; 6. the second of May; 7. the twenty-eighth of December; 8. the third of November; 9. the thirtieth of February; 10. the fourth of April; 11. the sixth of August; 12. the twenty-second of October; 13. the ninth of July; 14. the thirteenth of February

5

e	x	c	i	t	e	d
d	c	a	n	d	l	e
w	s	i	v	p	k	n
e	j	l	i	v	m	s
p	a	r	t	y	b	u
r	g	c	a	k	e	r
e	e	f	t	u	z	p
s	r	t	i	l	k	r
e	d	h	o	o	o	i
n	r	g	n	u	x	s
t	q	s	y	d	a	e

excited – aufgeregt; candle – Kerze; party – Fest; cake – Kuchen; present – Geschenk; invitation – Einladung; loud – laut; surprise – Überraschung

6 to invite; to dance; to laugh; to sing

7 I **live** in London Road.
I'd **like** to invite you to my party.
I **want** lots of presents.

8 *Mary:* Are you a good **cook?**
Chris: Yes, of course. OK. First, let's look for a **recipe.**
Mary: This looks good. Chocolate **cake.**
Chris: OK. Let's make that. What do we **need?**
Mary: We need two **eggs**, flour and **sugar.**
Chris: **How much** sugar do we need?
Mary: Er. 125 grams. And how many eggs have we got?
Chris: I don't know. Let's **count** them.

9 I want to buy a bag of **flour.**
We need a cup of **water.**
Have we got a box of **eggs?**
I want to eat **lots of** pizza.
Let's make a few **sandwiches.**
We've only got a little **sugar.**

10 Would you like to make a chocolate cake?
I want to eat lots of chocolate crispies.
Do you want to buy a sandwich?
I don't want to eat cheese sandwiches.

11 When would she like to have the party?
Who does she want to invite?
She wouldn't like to make a cake.

12 7th – the seventh; 12th – the twelfth; 21st – the twenty-first; 9th – the ninth; 2nd – the second; 32nd – the thirty-second

13 10.5.: the tenth of May/May the tenth
31.10.: the thirty-first of October/October the thirty-first
12.3.: the twelfth of March/March the twelfth
2.8.: the second of August/August the second

14
1. A man **is walking** his dog.
2. The dogs **are chasing** a ball.
3. She **is playing cards**.
4. You **are sitting on** a sofa.
5. We **are swimming**.
6. I **am making** a cake.

15
Are you making a cup of tea?
Are they dancing?
Is he trying on that sweatshirt?
Are we singing the right song?
Am I walking the right way?
Is she eating breakfast?

16
Is Christine dancing with Pete? – Yes, she is.
Are Alan and Robert watching TV? – Yes, they are.
Are you eating all the cake? – No, I'm not./No, we aren't.
Are we having a good time? – Yes, you are./Yes, we are.
Is Kyle laughing at me? – No, he isn't.
Is Jane waiting for me? – Yes, she is.

17
Susanne usually goes swimming on Saturday afternoon but today she **isn't swimming.** She **is/'s having** a birthday party in the garden. What **are the children doing** at her party? The girls **are playing** a game under the tree and the boys **are eating.**
Is Susanne having a good time? Yes, **she is. Are her parents helping** at the party? No, **they aren't.** But they **are watching** the birthday party.

18
1. No, they aren't. They are playing tennis.
2. No, she isn't. She's sleeping.
3. Yes, they are.
4. No, you aren't. You are driving a car.

19
zählbar: box, birthday, street, year
unzählbar: flour, help, homework, tea

20
Mum: Come on. We haven't got **much** time. What do we need?
Liam: Er, we haven't got **much** flour. And we haven't got **many** eggs.
Mum: Well, we only need **a few** eggs and **a little** flour so that's OK.
Liam: Have we got **much** chocolate? We need a lot or we can't make **many** chocolate crispies.
Mum: Yes, but we only need **a few** chocolate cripsies because nobody likes them.
Liam: What? But ... Oh, I see, it was a joke.

21 1. a bag of crisps; 2. a box of pencils; 3. a bag of apples; 4. a cup of tea; 5. a box of cornflakes; 6. a tin of cat food

22 a bag of mice
two tins of sand
three boxes of old shoes
a pound of candles

23 I find a book on the first day of April.
There's a house on the first page of the book.
The door of the house opens.
A photo of my family is in the house.

24 the girl's clothes
the colour of the tin
the cat's eyes
the first day of the second week

25 Beschreibung **C** stimmt mit dem Bild überein.

26
1. Because he wants to buy a present for his sister.
2. No, he doesn't.
3. Three.
4. It's too expensive.
5. Because he can't find a good book.
6. At half past five.

27
Is it Ann's birthday today? ↗
No, it's on the fifteenth of June. ↘
Have you got her a present? ↗
No, I haven't. ↘
What are you doing now? ↗
I'm making a present for Ann. ↘

28
1. A black sweatshirt.
2. Five pounds ninety-nine.
3. Large.
4. Extra large and medium.
5. Extra large.
6. No, he doesn't.
7. It's too big.

29 bars of chocolate: 55p; packets of crisps: 33p; dog magazine: £3.45; green apples: 40p for a pound; red apples: 89p for a bag; red bags: £3.15

30 They aren't swimming in the garden, they're dancing to a new CD.
Her parents aren't walking in the park, they're working in the garden.
John isn't playing cards in the bedroom, he's doing a card trick in the living room.
They haven't got sandwiches and chocolate cake, they've got pizzas, crisps, chocolate crispies and birthday cake.

Revision B (Unit 4 – 5)

1 1. recipe; 2. to invite; 3. transport; 4. to work; 5. left; 6. money

2

w	**e**	o	a	**p**	q	**j**
f	**a**	**m**	**o**	**u**	**s**	**u**
d	**s**	y	f	**b**	k	**m**
c	**y**	**m**	j	**l**	a	**b**
s	**p**	**e**	**c**	**i**	**a**	**l**
h	**e**	**d**	g	**c**	b	**e**
k	**a**	**i**	l	o	r	**d**
p	**s**	**u**	u	b	l	r
i	**y**	**m**	**r**	**i**	**c**	**h**

a **famous** castle; a **rich** man; a **special** cake; a **jumbled** sentence; **public** transport; an **easy-peasy** question; a **medium** T-shirt

3

1. Where do you live?
2. Do you like London?
3. What do you (usually) do in the evening?
4. What does your brother usually do?

4

Naomi: What do you want to buy?
Kate: I want to buy a book.
Naomi: But Lisa doesn't like books.
Kate: Yes, but she likes music and this book is about music.
Naomi: Does Lisa still play in a band?
Kate: Yes, she does but she doesn't play with her old band. She's got a new band.

5 Hi Ben. What **are you doing?** – **I'm sitting** in a café.
Are you eating your lunch? – No, **I'm not. I'm reading** a book.
And what **are your friends doing?** – Well, Kylie **is trying on** a sweatshirt in a clothes shop and Mark **is looking** at some CDs.
Are they looking for a present for their mum? – No, they **aren't looking for** a present. They haven't got any money.

6 Hi. It's **me,** Yvonne. Is Peter there? – Yes, **he** is.
Can I speak to **him?** – No, **you** can't because he's talking to Susan on his mobile.
Oh, **I** want to speak to **her,** too. – Well, why don't **you** come here and then you can speak to **them?** You only live up the road.

7
1. On Sunday.
2. Yes, he does.
3. Because he doesn't like swimming.
4. Because he hasn't got any money.
5. Because he makes great sandwiches.

8
A1: Excuse me. Have you got the new 4U CD?
B3: Oh, we only need a little.
A4: It's 10.50.
B2: Well, we've got eggs, flour and sugar, but how much chocolate do we need?
B1: OK. Have we got everything for the chocolate cake?
A2: Yes, we have. It's over there under the big poster.
A3: Oh, thank you. How much is it?
B4: What? I'm sure we need lots of chocolate.

9 Emma would like to make a cake but she only has a little flour and a few eggs. She goes shopping but the shops aren't open. Why? It's half past three in the morning and Emma is still sleeping.

10 A few people/children are having a birthday party. They've got a birthday cake and the girls are eating sandwiches. The boys are playing football and a cat is chasing a dog. A man is walking his dog and a woman is riding her bike.

Unit 6

1 Every year we like to go away
for a week or two's **holiday.**
I like to sit upon the **sand**
with an **ice-cream** in my hand.
I always go to the mile long **pier**
and play **arcade games** and often **hear**
the sound of waves upon the **rocks**
and see people playing with their dogs.
And then it's time for me to look
for my little old **address book**
because before my holiday ends
I must write **postcards** to my friends.

2 You can … **fly** a kite; **row** a boat; **pack** your bags; **climb** a mountain; **go surfing** on the sea; **build** a sand castle.

3

w	**c**	a	q	y	b	**l**	k
m	**o**	**u**	**n**	**t**	**a**	**i**	**n**
f	**a**	o	m	h	e	**g**	o
j	**s**	p	**s**	z	f	**h**	**h**
n	**t**	i	**e**	k	g	**t**	**a**
o	**c**	**e**	**a**	**n**	l	**h**	**r**
m	d	u	**s**	u	m	**o**	**b**
c	s	v	**i**	z	i	**u**	**o**
a	y	d	**d**	i	l	**s**	**u**
f	d	c	**e**	k	s	**e**	**r**
v	**i**	**l**	**l**	**a**	**g**	**e**	o

ocean – Ozean; mountain – Berg; village – Dorf; coast – Küste; seaside – Meeresküste; harbour – Hafen; lighthouse – Leuchtturm

4 What do you think **about/of** Penzance?
I need to look **up** that word in my dictionary.
I'm waiting **for** Ann again.
Can you take **off** your wellies before you go into the house, please?
I often read **to** my little sister.
Click **on** the picture for more information.
I'd like to get **into** the boat and sail to France.

5 Jahreszeit – season; Winter – winter; Frühling – spring; Sommer – summer; Herbst – autumn

6 When it's **windy,** you can fly a kite.
In the summer it's usually **warm.**
You don't lie on the beach when it's **cold.**
People often wear wellies when it **rains.**
You can't go surfing in a **storm** because the **wind** is too **strong.**
The rain **pitter-patters** on the window.

7 die – sterben; survive – überleben; ruin – zerstören; crash – zusammenstoßen; sink – untergehen

8 Can you **bring** me my wellies, please?
I always **take** my swimsuit on holiday.
Bring the ice-cream here, please.
Can you **take** him this souvenir?

9 We've got a pier **a** mile long.
There are lots of shops and cafés in the town **of** Penzance.
Jack is surfing **on** the Internet.
We often sing songs **on** the way home.

10 1. 130; 2. 2,013; 3. 40,208; 4. 66,092; 5. 570,611; 6. 1,711,218

11 1066 – ten sixty-six
1324 – thirteen twenty-four
1800 – eighteen hundred
1998 – nineteen ninety-eight
2000 – two thousand
2008 – two thousand and eight

12 *gewohnheitsmäßig:* 2., 4., 6., 8.
gerade ablaufend: 1., 3., 5., 7.

13

Martin:	Hi Graham. What **are you doing** now?
Graham:	I'**m going** to Cornwall on the train.
Martin:	Oh, yes. You **always go** to Cornwall on holiday.
Graham:	Yes, I know and we **always have** a good time but we **usually go** by car. It's terrible on the train.
Martin:	Why? I **like** trains.
Graham:	Yes, but you **don't go** with two little sisters. Listen! They'**re singing!** They **always sing** in the car.

14

Jane **gets up** at 8 o'clock and then **goes** downstairs. Usually Jane **doesn't get up** early on Saturday but today she'**s going** on holiday and she's excited. Her parents **are having** breakfast in the kitchen now but her brother and sister **are still sleeping.** Jane **eats** her breakfast, **washes** her face and then **packs** her bag. She's ready. She's so happy because this year she **isn't going** on holiday with her family, she'**s going** with her friend, Ann and Ann's family.

Just then the phone **rings** and her mum **answers** it. "I'm sorry, Jane, Ann's car **isn't working** this morning, so you can't go on holiday with them now. But don't worry, you can come with us."

Jane is not happy. And why is her mum so happy? She **looks** at her mum and her mum suddenly laughs, "No, it was just a joke. They'**re coming** here now so you can take your bags into the garden."

15

Excuse me. Have you got **any** postcards, please?
Yes, we've got **some** over there.
Have you got **any** wellies?
Yes, I've got **some** but I don't know where they are.
Are there **any** rocks in the sea here?
No, there aren't **any** here but there are **some** over there on that beach.
I'd like **some** chocolate now.
Well, you can't have **any**.

16

1. I'm sorry. We've got no swimsuits.
2. *nicht mit* no *möglich*
3. There are no lighthouses near here.
4. I know no famous people.

17

1. Can you see any people on the beach?
2. No, there aren't any people there.
3. But I can see some (people) on the pier.
4. And are there any arcade games on the pier?
5. Yes, I think there are some there.

18 days; hobbies; feet; teeth; diaries; fish; children; scarves

19 dictionaries; men; parties; scarf; woman; children; babies; thieves; boys; teeth; women; shelves

20 The thieves' bags are in their cars.
The children's bikes are red.
The babies' beds are small.
The women's shoes look old.
I don't know those people's names.

21 *Reihenfolge:* C, B, A, D; 1. richtig; 2. richtig

22
1. In the south of England.
2. No, there aren't.
3. You can get there by boat.
4. You can go shopping, visit the pier, row a boat, build sand castles and catch fish in the sea.
5. To the west of the island because it's usually windy there and the waves are usually big.

23 *mit* [ɜː]: girl, Germany, surf, survive, verb, person, word
ohne [ɜː]: warm, summer, harbour, adventure, storm, worry, hear, very

24
1. For a cousin.
2. She likes them but they're too expensive.
3. The bags are £8.50.
4. She likes surfing on the Internet.
5. £3.98

25 Our town is **in** the north of England and it's **1,850** years old. Lots of tourists come here every **summer** because it's a great place for **tourists.** There are **some** beautiful beaches near here and they are good for **children** because there aren't **any rocks** in the sea. Many **people,** old and young, love the interesting museums in our town. But remember! **Bring** your **scarf** with you in **winter** because it can be very **cold.**

26 Mark möchte nach **Llangollen,** Christine nach **Brighton.** Sie entscheiden sich für **Conway.**

Unit 7

1 1. pig; 2. monkey; 3. bird; 4. fox; 5. cow; 6. chicken

2 You can find cows and pigs on a **farm.**
Foxes and birds are **wild** animals.
You can see monkeys and tigers in a **zoo.**
You can ride a **horse.**
Cows and horses usually eat **grass** in a **field.**
Sheep usually live outside.

3 We **milk** the cows every morning.
I want to **muck out** the horses.
Pigs **stink** and they love it.
I always **look after** the baby animals when their mums don't want them.
Sometimes the pigs **fight over** the food.

4 1. hand; 2. leg; 3. ear; 4. eye; 5. foot; 6. face

5 to take a photo; to think of; to run after; to explain; to mend; to smile; to be right; to stand; to drink

6

w	f	**n**	**d**	z	u	**s**
c	**l**	**e**	**a**	**r**	m	**a**
w	**o**	**r**	**r**	**i**	**e**	**d**
d	y	v	**k**	j	**m**	t
e	n	**o**	d	g	**p**	e
a	i	**u**	r	c	**t**	p
d	l	**s**	x	n	**y**	r

besorgt – worried; traurig – sad; leer – empty; tot – dead; klar – clear; dunkel – dark; nervös – nervous

7 What must you do in the morning?
I must feed the chickens.
My dad must milk the cows.

8 Must you muck out the shed?
We must look after the horses.
You must bring the sheep home now.

9 When you buy a dog, you must look after it. You must give it good food and you **mustn't** give it chocolate every day. It's too sweet. You must walk your dog every day but you **needn't** walk for hours. One hour every day is enough. You must wash your dog but you **needn't** wash it in the bathroom – dogs get very dirty! And remember you **mustn't** get a dog if you are allergic to them.

10 Dogs mustn't run after sheep.
We needn't feed the cats.
Foxes mustn't eat the chickens.
You needn't ride the horses.

11 (In the morning) my dad milks the cows in the cow shed (in the morning).
(After breakfast) my mum feeds the chickens in the garden (after breakfast).
(At half past twelve) we all eat lunch in the kitchen (at half past twelve).
(In the summer) we often eat outside in the fields (in the summer).
(At night) we bring the sheep home (at night).
(At the weekend) children ride the horses in the fields (at the weekend).

12 Let's get up early and leave early.
Let's have breakfast before we leave.
We must take wellies because farms are always dirty.
Can you wear wellies when you ride a horse?
I like horses but I can't ride them.
I must take my mobile so I can phone Rob.

13 Let's go to the zoo and have lunch there.
No, we can't have lunch there because it's too expensive.
Well, let's make some sandwiches before we go to the zoo.
I like the zoo but there are always too many people there.
It's better when the weather's bad.
We can go in the monkey house when it rains.

14 Dogs are funny when you play with them.
Cats don't like dogs because dogs chase cats.
Cats eat cat food and they drink milk.

15 1. They get to the farm; 2. Chris is not happy; 3. Chris starts to like the farm; 4. Help for the dog; 5. Chris gets a pet

16
1. … sie sich um den Hund kümmert.
2. Dass man sie zweimal am Tag füttern muss.
3. Ein Buch über Hunde.
4. Ja, aber nicht allein.
5. Ja, zweimal am Tag, auch bei Regen.

17 I've got a camera but I can't take good photos.

I don't need a camera because I can take photos with my mobile.

I want a video camera so that I can make short films.

18 I work at the **zoo** and **it's** a great job. I **needn't** start work until nine o'clock but I **usually** get to the zoo at about eight **and** then I say hello to the **animals.** They are like friends. First I **must** feed them. I always talk to the animals **when** I feed them. **They** like that. They **don't** answer, of course, **but** sometimes I think that they know what I'm saying.
I always play with the **monkeys** when I see **them.** Monkeys love games and I **think** they can **laugh,** too. Then I often **ride** the elephants. The elephants **need** a walk and I love riding them. Elephants are funny, **too,** but you **must** watch out with elephants **because** they can hurt you. I don't play with all the animals, of **course.** For example, I **mustn't** go **too** near a tiger.

19 1. true; 2. false; 3. true; 4. true; 5. false; 6. true

20
[æ]: animal, activity, hand, bad
[eɪ]: same, bacon, take, famous
[ɑː]: farm, grass, half, dark

Revision C (Unit 6 – 7)

1 family: grandad; half-sister; parents
people with jobs: farmhand; teacher; vet
other people: tourist; visitor; woman
farm animals: cow; pig; sheep
pets: cat; dog; mouse

2 calm – nervous: ruhig – nervös; right – wrong: richtig – falsch; long – short: lang – kurz; good – bad: gut – schlecht; boring – interesting: langweilig – interessant; large – small: groß – klein; happy – sad: glücklich – traurig; great – terrible: toll – schrecklich; cheap – expensive: billig – teuer; loud – quiet: laut – leise

3 I'd like to live **on** a farm and I often think **about/of** my holidays there. Before I go to the farm, I always take **off** my shoes and try **on** my old wellies. You need wellies on a farm because it's always dirty. When I get **to** the farm, I always go and look **for** Shep, the old dog. He's my friend and he always asks **for** a biscuit. In the morning I always wake **up** early and then I look **after** the chickens. Sometimes I muck **out** the pigs, too, but never before breakfast. The pigs are funny, I think. They always fight **over** their breakfast. When I'm at home, I always talk **about** the farm to my friends. Sometimes I want to run **away** and go to the farm again but I know that I must go to school. But when I'm 16 …

4 schon – already; erste/r/s – first; nächste/r/s – next; später – later; im Augenblick – just now; bevor – before; sofort – right now; alle (zehn Tage) – every (ten days); immer – always; nie – never; manchmal – sometimes; oft – often

5 I often play tennis **at** the weekend.
School finishes **at** half past three.
I always get up late **on** Saturday.
What do you usually do **in** the evening?
What's **on** TV now?
I like to sit **on** the beach **in** summer.
I usually walk **from** home **to** school.

6 How are you? – I'm fine, thanks.
I like Jim. He's great fun.
What time is it, please? – It's five thirty.
That's one pound fifty, please. – Here you are.
Look at your room! What a mess!
John's not happy. He's fed up.
I don't like my brother. He's a pain.
Where are you from? – London.

7
Rob: Have you **got** any sisters, Janet?
Janet: No, I **haven't** but **I've** got a brother. His name **is** Tony.
Rob: Oh, how old **is** he?
Janet: **He's** twenty-two. And **he's** got two children.
Rob: So **you're** an aunt and **you're** only twelve! How old **are** his children?
Janet: **They're** one and three. They **aren't** very interesting.

8 Look! What are those birds doing?
They're waiting for some food.
They always come here on Saturdays.
Why do they come here on Saturdays?
Because my mum doesn't cook at the weekend.

9
1. I always get up early because I needn't go to school.
2. We often have breakfast in the garden when it's warm.
3. We usually go to Scotland in summer.
4. My brother never swims in the sea because it's too cold.
5. It doesn't get dark in Scotland until 11 o'clock.

10 A dog's life is great. I **can** get up late and I **needn't** go to school. I **can** sleep when I want and eat when I'm hungry. I **must** look after the house and I **mustn't** break things but I **can** sleep on the sofa. And at the weekend I **can** watch Chris play tennis in the park, but I **can't** play, of course. And I **mustn't** chase the ball, says Chris.

11
Nina: We've got **a few** cheese sandwiches but have we got **any** crisps?
David: Yes, we've got **some** crisps but we haven't got **any** apples.
Nina: OK. Here you are. Oh, and we haven't got **much** chocolate.
David: No, we must buy **some.** And we've only got **a little** water.
Nina: There's **some** here. But we've got **no** tins of cola.
David: Well, we don't need **many** tins. I don't like it. Is that everything?
Nina: Oh no. What about our clothes?

12 My uncle's house is over there.
The name of the house is Seaview.
My cousins' bikes are in the garden.
On the first day of the holidays they always go to the beach.

13 *Hotelformular:*
Name of visitor: Ann Jennings
Phone number: 0161 534 2891
Dates: From 2nd August to 13th August
Anns Notizzettel:
Price of room: 63.50 a night or 420 pounds a week
Number of rooms: 132
At hotel: Swimming pool, garden
Address: 6, Church Road, Bamburgh
Hotel closes at half past ten.

14 Hi Jenny,
Would you like to visit me in August? It's doesn't often rain in summer so we can go swimming in the sea every day. We usually take picnics to the beach in the summer and at the weekend we often sail in my dad's boat. Please come! It's great fun here in August.
Lili

15 Usually two men/farmhands milk the cows and a woman feeds the hens. A/The cat usually chases some/the mice and the sheep usually eat grass in the field.
Today the hens are watching TV. The cat and mice are reading a book together and the sheep are playing football. One/A cow is playing the guitar and the other cows are listening. And why? Because the men/farmhands are sleeping under a tree.

16 1. true; 2. false; 3. true; 4. false; 5. true

Mit Green Line lernen wie es MIR passt!

Die Green Line Materialien sorgen für mehr Abwechslung und für gute Noten.

Workbook mit Audio-CD und Lernsoftware

ISBN 978-3-12-547128-3

ohne Lernsoftware

ISBN 978-3-12-547125-2

Arbeitsheft, Audio-CD und eine super Lernsoftware sichern den Erfolg.

Fit für Tests und Klassenarbeiten

ISBN 978-3-12-547201-3

Gezielte Vorbereitung auf Klassenarbeiten. So wird der nächste Test ganz easy.

Vokabellernheft

ISBN 978-3-12-547108-5

Alle Vokabeln des Schülerbuchs im praktischen Taschenformat mit Übungen und Lösungen.

Vokabel-Lernbox

ISBN 978-3-12-924008-3

Das gesamte Vokabular des Schülerbuchs auf Lernkarten. Fürs schnelle, dauerhafte und gründliche Lernen.

It's Green Line Time.

Die Green Line Materialien sind im Buchhandel erhältlich. Weitere Informationen zu Green Line unter www.klett.de.

Damit gibt's gute Noten

KomplettWissen Gymnasium Deutsch
mit CD-ROM
5. – 8. Schuljahr
ISBN 978-3-12-926032-6

KomplettWissen Gymnasium Mathematik
mit CD-ROM
5. – 8. Schuljahr
ISBN 978-3-12-926033-3

KomplettWissen Gymnasium Englisch
mit CD-ROM
5. – 8. Schuljahr
ISBN 978-3-12-926034-0

380 Kurztests die wirklich helfen Englisch
5./6. Schuljahr
ISBN 978-3-12-927155-1

Turbo Teacher Englisch 5. Schuljahr
Gymnasium
mit Audio-CD
ISBN 978-3-12-927188-9

380 Kurztests

In 15 Minuten besser werden: die optimale Lernmotivation für jeden Tag. Kleine Lernportionen in drei verschiedenen Schwierigkeitsstufen – geeignet für jede Schulform. Mit ausführlichen Lösungen zu jedem Kurztest.

Turbo Teacher

Lernen, was man wirklich braucht.
Ein Diagnosetest online oder im Buch für den Leistungs-Check. Das passgenaue Übungsprogramm abgestimmt auf den individuellen Bedarf führt schnell zu guten Noten. Anschauliche Erklärungen zeigen, wie's geht. Zahlreiche Übungsaufgaben mit ausführlichen Lösungen schaffen Sicherheit und Abschlusstests überprüfen den Lernerfolg.

Im Buchhandel erhältlich.

Weitere Informationen unter www.klett.de/lernhilfen